Vice Cop

TO

Vicar

A Journey of Faith and Healing

DERRICK WILKS WITH ANN WILKS

malcolm down
PUBLISHING

Grandchildren are a real blessing.

It has been a delight to see our two grandsons get excited about this project by asking questions and recounting these stories to their friends.

This book is for you, Noah and Josiah.

Contents

PART FOUR: Policeman to Pastor

Prologue

Have you ever made a stupid decision that almost cost you your life?

The sunlight sparkled off the surface and I breathed, basking in the warm air. I realised I had never seen water so clear and inviting. We were in Pensacola, Florida with all our diving gear in tow. I was with my wife, Ann, our daughter Rachel and her American husband, Justin, and we decided a dive together was the perfect way to spend Ann's fiftieth birthday. But of course, like all best laid plans, things were not straightforward; the weather forecast was dreadful with high winds and storms so unfortunately, deep-sea diving was off. However, we found a freshwater diving site – a grand alternative.

Set in a warm freshwater spring, with thousands of gallons rushing through it daily, there was a small dive shop where we could rent tanks and provide Justin with extra gear as he was a beginner. The water was amazingly clear and warm with fish and turtles surrounding us. Justin got into the water as we took time assembling and testing the equipment thoroughly, being watched by other divers sitting out in the sun.

Justin enjoyed a few minutes snorkelling before he accidentally dropped his snorkel into the water as he was getting out. It gently drifted down until it came to a rest not far away. I was the first to assemble all my kit and as I waited for Rachel and Ann, I made a fateful decision.

A diver should never dive alone.

But the sun was shining, the water was shallow and crystal clear, and I could see the snorkel just a few metres below the surface. So I slipped into the water and swam down to recover it. I love diving. Breathing through the regulator and hearing my inhales of breath through the mouthpiece is spectacular. I could never get enough of that.

Swimming down, I was alone in this huge spring. I could see to the bottom with the sun glinting down from above. I saw where the spring water entered the pond from a large hole and I watched the shoals of fish swim against the gentle current. It was idyllic. I soon located the missing snorkel; it had washed into a small cave at the steep side of the pond. The only problem was the cave was deeper than I thought so I couldn't quite reach in. I wriggled myself into the hole so I could grab it. That was when I realised, I was stuck. The large steel air bottle on my back was wedged on something I couldn't see. So, there I was, head and shoulders into a small cave with my feet flapping around. I couldn't turn my body and all I could see was about two feet in front of me.

Hey, but it was a lovely day. I was feeling great. Stuck, but great. I decided I could get myself out of this. All I had to do was release the tank and BCD (buoyancy control device) and swim out – simple. However, as I started to undo the clips and Velcro belts, I caught my regulator and knocked it from my mouth. As the regulator is the mouthpiece that allows me to breathe, I was now stuck in a hole with no air supply. I couldn't move and I couldn't see where the regulator had gone. I felt like a cork in a bottle.

'Funny place to die,' was all I could think.

Holding my breath felt like hours when it was less than a few minutes. Surprisingly, I didn't panic. I just hung there, and *it just so happened* that my regulator wafted back to my face. I was able to reach it and start breathing again. By that time, Ann was in the water and came to my rescue. It was a close thing and stupid and entirely my fault. Diving is inherently dangerous wherever we are, whether deep inside a Second World War wreck in the Red Sea or a few metres down in clear freshwater in Florida.

I was protected that day. Like I had been many times before.

PART ONE

Foundations

Chapter One

Faith, Love and a Purpose

As a boy, I would watch Jacques Cousteau on the black-and-white television; he was exploring the silent world of the deep. Lying in the bath at night, I'd submerge my head beneath the water, breathing through the rubber shower attachment that we'd connect to the taps for washing our hair. I don't remember much of my childhood, but I do know it was nothing like the life children have now. We had more freedom and no electronic gadgets to drag us into any other world but our own.

I was brought up in Driffield, a small market town in East Yorkshire. My parents had working-class backgrounds, and both worked two jobs to get food on the table. One of their jobs was working at the local bar, and sometimes I managed to stay awake long enough to hear my dad coming home with a bag of chips. Occasionally, I was allowed to share them. This was during the late 1950s and early 1960s when we had no car, no phone in the house and no central heating. I remember winter mornings when I could write my name in the frost on the inside of my bedroom window. Entertainment was extremely limited; we had a black-and-white television set with a choice of only two channels. So, I made my own entertainment by cycling almost everywhere, especially on the weekends.

I passed my eleven-plus and went to the local grammar school in nearby Bridlington. Having to catch the bus every day, I remember we would play cards to pass the time. We even had to attend on a Saturday morning to make up for Wednesday afternoons, which were devoted to sport and the Combined Cadet Force (CCF). I joined the RAF side of the CCF, learning how to march, care for my uniform, shoot a gun and even fly a plane. The school had its own shooting range where I would often practise on a lunchtime becoming quite the marksman; I was a natural with the .22 rifle.

We travelled regularly to an RAF base in Lincolnshire where we were taught to fly two-seater Chipmunks. Walking out to the plane is such an unpleasant memory; the parachute was strapped under my bum, making me walk like a duck. That was the only downside, though. Once in the plane, the pilot would take off and then hand the controls to us.

'You have control,' he would say.

'I have control, sir,' was the reply.

At first, we learnt to fly in a straight line, which is not as easy as it sounds. The slightest movements on the joystick or the rudder pedals would see the plane bouncing all over the sky. As we got more proficient the pilot did acrobatics, showing us how to perform manoeuvres and then allowing us to learn the loop-the-loop and barrel rolls. I can still remember the drop in my stomach when performing a stall turn when the plane had climbed almost vertically up until eventually it just hangs there in the air. That is the moment when the pilot pushes the stick right over, taking the nose down with a massive acceleration as it drops into a sharp downward dive. Oh, the thrill of it all. By the time I was in the sixth form I was the head cadet in the CCF and was involved in training the younger boys coming up.

Overall, life was good but that didn't mean I wasn't easily misled. I would often go down to the local pub and sit opposite my dad working behind the bar. He would always buy me a pint and set it on the bar between us saying, 'If anyone comes along, tell them it's mine.' When I worked a Saturday job in the local supermarket, it didn't take me long to work out that I could help myself from the cash register to supplement my wages. I was also studying chemistry for A-Level and so a friend and I got into making homemade fireworks. It wouldn't have been a surprise if any of these things had escalated and led me down darker paths.

When I was seventeen, a young teenage girl came in one Saturday and asked if she could leave some invitations to a concert at my till so customers could help themselves. Without giving it much thought, I grunted an 'I suppose so', and hardly gave them a second glance. I was feeling miserable that day; my girlfriend had dumped me and life seemed to be going nowhere.

Towards the end of the day, as I was tidying up my cash desk to leave, I picked up what was left of the invitations and gave them a proper look. They were typed out on scruffy bits of paper, had been cut out by hand, and were not the most inspiring bit of publicity I had ever seen. Despite that, I learnt about a concert at the local Women's Institute hall for a band of young musicians called The Advocates who would be coming from Lincolnshire to perform for free. I was interested in music. For years I had listened to Radio Caroline and other illegal radio stations on a tiny crystal radio set that I hooked up to the metal springs on my mattress to get better volume. Perhaps some live music would cheer me up a bit and the fact the event was free tipped the balance. I would give it a go.

The hall was only a ten-minutes' walk from home and after dinner I set off, but when I was almost at the door, I chickened out. I walked back home, feeling more miserable so I decided to go back again. The same thing happened, but this time as I walked towards my house, I felt compelled to go back to the hall. I had almost reached the very place where I had turned around the first time when the music started: loud, catchy, and the sort of stuff I liked. I opened the door and quietly slipped into a seat on the back row.

At first, I was too busy listening to the music and watching the band, who were not much older than me, to even be aware of my surroundings but I soon noticed I was by far the youngest person there. The other people, and there were not many of them, were all as old as my parents, and some were positively ancient. At that moment a band member began to talk. He simply explained how he felt that his life had no meaning or purpose until someone told him Jesus could radically change his life. He had started following Jesus from then on and dedicated his life to telling others that following Jesus was the best decision he ever made. It made me think. I wondered if Jesus could make a difference for me too. When they said the band were playing at the church the next day, I decided I would go along and hear more. The tiny church they attended was only a few hundred yards from my home, so once I had started walking, there wasn't time to change my mind.

Once again, the music was great and the guys were talking about following Jesus and once again, I felt the tug; it all seemed so real for them. Could it be real for me? The following week they had another couple of musicians booked, so I planned to go with some trepidation. If there was one place in town I didn't want to go, it was the youth centre at the secondary school. As mentioned, I was a grammar school boy who was often mocked and ridiculed by the local lads. However, that day was worth the trip. The band was great, but the Australian singer-songwriter, Len Magee, who was a former drug addict, impressed me the most. His story of freedom from addiction by the power of Jesus was mind-blowing, undeniable and a testimony to the transformation that following Jesus can do for anyone. I knew it was what I needed. So, on April Fool's Day 1973, I gave my heart to Jesus, asking him to forgive all my past and give me a new start. I didn't understand all the theology, but I knew he had become my Lord and my Saviour. It was the best decision I have ever made.

That little church down the road from my house became my second home. I have mentioned that music was an important part of my life. I had started to learn the guitar. Although I could only play three chords, I wasn't content with the low volume on my acoustic guitar, so I glued a pick-up from an old record player inside the sound hole and played it through an amplifier. Very soon the young pastor had me singing and playing at the front of the church. We usually had twenty minutes worth of songs before the service started and a good group of young people got regularly involved. It wasn't long before we got together as a band: a couple of guitars, a lead singer and some backing vocals. The church people were happy to encourage us. I used an amplifier from the church's reel-to-reel cinema projector for the guitar and we built a reputation among the youth groups in the area for talking about Jesus and singing secular songs with altered lyrics.

Of course, we needed a band name and we chose The Disciples, which really sums up my faith. I had never thought of faith in terms of attending church, but of being a follower of Jesus. I still do. He had transformed my life and I wanted to be involved in telling other people about him, so that he could transform their lives too.

One evening, we were invited to the Baptist church in Bridlington. One of our backing vocalists was amazed to see her school friend Ann sitting at the back of the hall. Ann had been brought up in one of the cults and was vocal about her beliefs in the classroom. In fact, her friends would have said if someone in their circle of friends was to have become a Christian, it would be anyone except Ann. Despite that, my friend asked her if she would like to come to our next concert up the coast in Staithes, a beautiful fishing village. It would mean she would have to stay over at her house. Ann agreed and came from school that Friday with her overnight bag.

It was now November and the church allowed us to use their minibus, which had no heating. It was certainly chilly on the way there, but on our return, it was positively freezing. It just so happened that I was sitting in the back of the van next to Ann. She was soon shivering. So, what did I do, the gentleman that I am? I took off my jacket and put it around her shoulders. Well, that was that! The beginning of a wonderful relationship that has led to more than forty-five years of marriage.

For Ann and me, it was certainly an exciting time, but my parents were not in the least bit pleased. It was A-Level year and their plan was for me to go to university – something they had not been able to do. They were furious when my grades were not nearly as good as everyone had been expecting; inevitably, Ann and I had been spending more time together than perhaps we should have. I had asked her to marry me after we'd been dating for only a few weeks and we were still in school. I remember showing my mum the ring on her hand at my eighteenth birthday party. That went down like a lead balloon.

My grades meant it wouldn't be possible to fulfil my parents' dream, but it just so happened that Ann's mum was a teacher and she had soon found a place for me to complete a three-year Diploma in Applied Chemistry at Sheffield. The polytechnic was thirty miles from Huddersfield School of Music where Ann was to be studying. We were engaged for four and a half years. It was not easy to keep in touch in the days before mobile phones. I remember going to the phone box with a pile of change and ringing up the hall of residence where Ann lived. Someone would answer it and then go running through the hall shouting for Ann. Sometimes my money would run out before she even got to the phone. Those were the days.

I threw myself wholeheartedly into college life, eventually becoming the chairman of the Christian Union. One of the things I loved was putting on some of the best Christian bands in the Students' Union venue; I was still determined to get the message of Jesus out in whatever way I could.

When it was my final year, all my coursemates were struggling to find jobs, worrying like mad about those dreaded finals and generally panicking about their future, but not me. You see, a few months previously there was a burglary in my student digs. The thief hadn't got away with much of great value, but then again, students didn't own much of anything. That meant the little he had taken was worth reporting to the authorities, who called in the police.

That led to one of the most tedious afternoons ever. A burly police officer was sitting in my only chair, drinking tea from my only mug as I perched on the bed to give my statement. He slowly retrieved his notebook from deep inside his pocket, pulling out his pencil, which he licked before writing down the date and time on the next clean page.

Peering over his spectacles he said, 'Now then, lad, let's start agen at 't beginning,' in a broad Yorkshire accent. After he had taken copious notes, he took out a Witness Statement Form and began to slowly and laboriously copy out everything we had just talked about. It was while he was meticulously transcribing it that I felt a voice within me simply say, 'You could do that.' Totally out of the blue, as I was willing the policeman to leave so I could get on with my life, the voice was so clear, 'You could do that – you could do it better than that – what's hard about that?'

In the Christian Union some of the guys and I had been discussing whether God would speak to us today. One friend said that often when he was reading his Bible, a word or phrase would almost jump off the page and he began to realise that was how God spoke to him. I had noticed this too. One of the other guys remembered reading a verse in Isaiah which says, 'Your ears will hear a voice behind you, saying, "This is the way; walk in it"' (Isaiah 30:21). He said that he sometimes felt a prompting to do something. So, that day as I watched the police officer writing his notes, I knew the thought that dropped into my mind was God speaking to me about my future career. This was not the first time I'd heard his voice and I was beginning to recognise it as the voice of God. Over the next few days that thought kept coming back to me, time and time again: 'You could do that!' The police never caught the thief nor found my five-pound note, but I had discovered a new purpose for my life.

At that time, the police were almost a military institution and underpaid so it didn't attract educated personnel. This being the case, the two recruiting officers who came to my home a few weeks later were amazed that a well-educated young man, who was a committed Christian, would even think of applying. In fact, they tried hard to dissuade me from carrying on with the process. There was an entrance examination, but because I had passed my A-Levels, I didn't even need to take it, and so while my peers were panicking at the end of term, I was simply confident my life was going in the right direction.

I know my parents didn't agree. After all, it was not the job with good career prospects they had envisaged for their son. Personally, I had never thought about joining the police before, but after hearing that voice, I couldn't shake the certainty that this was God's guiding hand directing my future.

Chapter Two

Rats

30 August 1977. The big day. With a handful of other PCs (Police Constables), I marched briskly into one of those ancient buildings in Hull that had survived the Second World War bombing raids: Hull Crown Court. Here I was sworn in as a constable of Humberside Police, sworn to serve and protect Her Majesty the Queen and the people of the United Kingdom. I received my uniform and had my hair cut, then I went to Dishforth for ten weeks of intensive training. During that time, the scruffy student became the smart PC with a slick new haircut, boots so bulled you could see your face in them and trousers creased to a knife-edged sharpness.

A few months later I was walking down the road between the deserted ancient warehouses of the old town. It was the darkest part of the night. I watched carefully as my torch beam moved endlessly from left to right, searching. For what? The rats, of course.

I've always had a thing about rats. Perhaps it started with my dad's stories about the war-torn city of Hull, apparently the most bombed city in the country. Growing up there, he had seen things. Like most people who had survived the war, he didn't talk about all he had seen, but he did tell me about the rats – thousands of the things, racing off the grain ships when they docked. They scurried down the streets, their claws scratching and scraping along pavements as they hunted out new places to hide.

So, this night – one of my first night shifts as a young twenty-one-year-old copper – I was on foot patrol down the streets of Hull, alone, and I admit it, scared. I was hoping that I'd learn not to be.

I was soon forced to learn as colleagues had a novel way of weeding out the faint-hearted. Policing wasn't for wimps and a few nights later I was walking the same beat, approaching the corner of a dark alleyway when I came across an old man crouched in a doorway, mumbling and groaning. Gingerly, I walked over to him.

'Er? Are you alright, sir?'

He leapt to his feet and grabbed me by the throat. I was terrified, until he started laughing. He was another police officer, wearing a face mask and an old coat. Such pranks were not uncommon, just a way to toughen up the newbies; but today, the practice is frowned upon. Colleagues could help with the learning process, but life experiences would teach me even greater lessons.

I had only been in 'the job' three or four days when I was beaten up for the first time. It was the end of my shift at midday and I was still in uniform. I was waiting for the bus on Ferensway to take me to my new digs. Three drunk teenagers came to the bus stop, at first content to mock me and push me around; they soon turned to thumping me, eventually leaving me bruised, battered and knocked to the floor before they ran away laughing and flaunting my helmet. What a trophy that was for them, and what an embarrassment for me to explain to a senior officer. The whole incident, though humiliating, left me determined never to lose again. I think in all my years of service I only once lost a prisoner, but that is a story for another time.

By 1977, Ann had moved to Leeds University to do a one-year Diploma in Education. We were married a year later at Bridlington Priory. One of our wedding hymns was 'Take My Life and Let It Be' by Frances Ridley Havergal (1836–79). It was written more than a hundred years ago by a blind lady. She could have been bitter about her life, and yet she wasn't. She wrote many wonderful hymns that have been a blessing to many people. This one lists the many blessings the Lord gives to us: moments, days, voice, intellect, hands and feet, and it encourages us to give each one back to him to use for his glory. Ann always reminds me that on our wedding day we consciously sang and meant each word. Over the years we have seen how God took us at our word and has used our giftings to bring glory to him.

When we got married, we were glad that the police had houses, as we couldn't save for a deposit on a mortgage. Our first house was on Bransholme, the largest council estate in Europe at the time. The police rented a few mid-terraced houses and offered us one. It had three bedrooms, a kitchen diner and a small lounge which led out to the back lawn. The house had been previously occupied by a policeman who wasn't popular in the area. One day a local thug had thrown a wooden stake through the door when he answered it.

It wasn't the most salubrious place to start married life, yet we were happy there. Our first baby was born there and, before long, we ran a small kids' club on a Friday night with a dozen neighbourhood children; they would come to our house and listen, spellbound, to exciting stories. We used flannelgraph cut-out pictures attached to big colourful boards to tell the stories and we all had such fun. Music had always been a big part of our lives, including in these clubs, and I mean it was a big part. I play guitar and Ann had a Bechstein grand piano, and with that in our lounge there was only room for two comfy chairs. It's a good thing the kids from the club liked sitting on the floor. Slowly but surely, we settled into life in the city.

However, we were always short of money; I remember only having a fifty-pence piece to give Ann for the shopping and scraping together five pounds for Christmas when the children were small. Regardless, we made the best of what we had.

So began my life as a police officer, with the understanding that one day God would call me back out. Psalm 23 is familiar to many and even in my darkest days of the oncoming illness I knew he was with me, taking me 'through the valley', and preparing his provision for the wide-open spaces he was 'leading me' into.

Chapter Three

Village Life

It was autumn 1980 and we were so excited. This village was to be our new home. We drove slowly around its streets, stopping frequently to admire the old houses as the stream flowed alongside the road. There was a charming old church, a pub and a post office; everything seemed to bode well for the next chapter in our lives. The anticipation was palpable in the car as we headed for my parents' home a few miles away to share the wonderful news.

Mum and Dad were both at work, so we let ourselves in and Ann made the coffee. In her childhood home, they only ever used a freestanding whistling kettle placed on the gas oven to boil. My mum, however, had an electric kettle. For some reason (perhaps it was in her excitement) Ann filled Mum's kettle, popped it on the stove and lit the gas ring beneath it. She walked into the lounge for a chat because, of course, the kettle would whistle once the water was boiling. However, it was not a whistling kettle that forced us both into the kitchen moments later, but the awful smell of burning plastic as the bottom of the kettle melted and dripped over the top of the oven. Unfortunately, the state of her kitchen was the thing my mum remembered of that day, not our exciting news about a new home.

Transitioning from a student to a PC had been a sharp learning curve. We often have the image of a PC donning a high-vis jacket, stab vest and an array of offensive tools such as pepper sprays, tasers, asps, and in some cases firearms and semi-automatic rifles. In my day we wore a black surge uniform, which was not waterproof, the obligatory 'noddy' hat that never fit properly, a cape, Doc Martin boots, and we carried a pair of handcuffs and a wooden truncheon. I was forever in trouble for the creases in my trousers not being sharp enough, my jacket never being brushed through, and my boots were never bulled sufficiently.

Yet, in those first three years, I had learnt the skills needed to be a good PC – to run towards danger, to deal with violent drunks and the frequent shoplifters. I would get hurt, but I had to shake it off like a boxer because, after all, as a PC, I was Superman. I spent my first two years walking the beat and the third year behind the wheel of panda cars, after a ten-week driving course. It was my expectation to stay in Hull for the remainder of my service.

So, it was quite the surprise when I was called into the inspector's office and was asked about transferring to a rural beat, in a village I had never heard of, in a district I had never visited . . . and, of course, I said yes. Much later, as I processed that time, I was reminded of Abraham in the book of Genesis. God called him out of a city full of false idols and called him to follow him to a new land, a land that he didn't know (Genesis 12). Just as the Lord had plans and purposes for Abraham, I believe he has plans for us too. All we must do is listen to his voice and follow his leadings, even when they surprise us. Rural beats were never given to a PC with only three years' experience; they were reserved for those up for promotion.

All this led to one beautiful autumn day when Ann and I and our little baby, Philip, loaded our things into a removal van and drove to the village of Wilberfoss on the outskirts of York. We moved into a lovely detached, red-brick, three-bedroom house. The police office was built onto the side of the house, accessed through an internal door off our living room.

The office contained a desk, chair, telephone and a large walk-in cupboard containing all sorts of paperwork I had never seen before. This included stacks of brown A4 forms marked 'Pig Movement Orders' (these were required during the swine vesicular disease outbreaks years previously). There were shotgun renewal forms and firearms certificates as most of the local farmers and landowners had guns; they would hold frequent pheasant shoots in the autumn and winter. It was traditional for them to invite the local bobby to act as a beater. They were great days out, walking through the woodland, disturbing the birds, and making them easy for the shooters to hit. It was not uncommon to come home to a brace of pheasants hanging on our back door, a generous gift from an anonymous source.

Our house was set in its own grounds, with an overgrown vegetable garden and hedges covered with the juiciest brambles. There were coal bunkers for the fire in the lounge and the anthracite that we needed for the central heating. The windows were made of lead frames and small panes, and tissue paper was tucked into the frames to keep out the drafts; we certainly needed them that winter. There was a garage, something we hadn't had in Hull, and a panda car, a 955cc Fiesta, for my personal use.

That first morning I put on my uniform, had breakfast, and took my coffee through to the office. I was at work, so what did I do now? So began an idyllic life and one of the most satisfying times of my career. It was a totally new lifestyle, as I was responsible for the policing of 150 square miles bordering North Yorkshire and containing more than eight small villages.

I was solely responsible for everything that went on: minor crimes in the villages, local domestic arguments and people producing traffic documents. I dealt with it all. I felt like the local sheriff in those cowboy films I loved. I certainly learnt to talk offenders down, as it would take twenty minutes for another officer to arrive for back up, most likely from the North Yorkshire Constabulary.

And so we settled into two years of the gentle, rural life. In some ways, it was like the television show, *Heartbeat*, which incidentally was set in the beautiful North Yorkshire Moors, less than an hour's drive from us. Ann and I were both involved in this new life. Often when I was out, she would take down people's details, or if I ever needed back-up, she would ring the local police station or 999 if necessary. One day she rang for help as I tried to talk down a guy who threatened to cut his own throat with a broken milk bottle, right on our front lawn.

Stargazing became a regular pastime; they were much more visible there than they were in Hull. We'd gaze and feel grateful for the new life we had. There is a beautiful psalm which says, 'When I consider your heavens, the work of your fingers, the moon and stars, which you have set in place, what is man that you are mindful of him, the son of man that you care for him?' (Psalm 8:3-4).

We knew that the Lord is an amazing creator and we felt so blessed that he cared for us and had brought us to this peaceful, rural village.

But one night, the peace and quiet was shattered by a loud mechanical voice next to our bed repeating the words, 'Alarm, garden centre!' The clock read 2 a.m. and I bolted out of bed, pulled on my trousers, and left the house as Ann picked up the phone to call for back-up.

To explain, across the main road from Wilberfoss, there was a garden centre occupying a large area of land. Over recent months, it had experienced a few burglaries. There was never a lot taken, just loose change and the contents of the charity box at the till. This was reported to me every week or so, which suggested someone local to the village was the burglar. The area was too big for me to watch constantly so I devised a trap. Before the days of internet and mobile phones, I improvised a solution. I put in a temporary alarm, which transmitted a radio signal to a scanner that we had installed at the side of our bed. The scanner had been in action for a couple of weeks before it was activated in the early hours that night. Ann rang for back-up and explained what was going on, although we knew there was likely to be a twenty-minute wait before the nearest officer would arrive.

I drove, with my lights off, to the front of the garden centre, jumped out and shone my torch through the greenhouses. I was able to make out the figure of a man. Unfortunately, he saw me just as I saw him. He set off running straight through the greenhouse wall, shattering the glass, which cascaded everywhere. I set off after him. Recognising him as a man from the village who lived down the road from the pub, I watched him run through a second glass wall, and off into the darkness, intending to make his escape. At that moment a police car arrived, with an officer who was a dog handler. He soon had his dog out and a few minutes later the three of us tracked the offender over the main road, down a narrow ginnel to the man's front door.

When he opened the door, he was covered in small cuts.

'How did you get those?' I asked him. He said it was from shaving. I arrested him for burglary and took him to Goole Police Station for processing; the owner of the garden centre was another satisfied customer.

We had been in Wilberfoss just two years when there was a reorganisation of the rural beats. The Wilberfoss police house was closed and the area it covered was split between Stamford Bridge and Bubwith. It just so happened that the PC at Stamford Bridge joined the team in Pocklington, so I could move from Wilberfoss to take on the extended area of Stamford Bridge, just eight miles away.

The police house at Stamford Bridge was in the middle of the village, right opposite the school and the Anglican church. There was a large front garden, set down to lawn and herbaceous borders; the drive was on the left-hand side of the property, leading straight up to the garage and the office door. The accommodation had a front entrance hall, with the lounge on the left boasting a beautiful open fire, a dining room and two reception rooms with large windows overlooking the enclosed front garden. The property was surrounded by seven-foot-high hedges and so was extremely private. The kitchen was at the back, leading to an outhouse that contained the oil-fired boiler for the central heating and opened inside to an old coalhouse and toilet. Two doors led outside, the one on the right to a tiny enclosed, over-grown area, and the other to the back garden with lawn, washing line and coal bunker. It was a fabulous place to bring up the children; we had Philip, a toddler and baby Rachel. We kept chickens in the over-grown area at the side of the house. Five hens laid sufficient eggs for all of us. However, as we would find out, this idyllic lifestyle was good at hiding the darker side of human nature.

PART TWO

The Ups and Downs

Chapter Four

Hill and Vale

A gentle breeze stirred the wildflowers in the meadow before me. Delicate blue harebells danced in the air waves, the brilliant scarlet of the poppies positively glowed in the early evening sun and the occasional, rare bee-orchids dared to show themselves among the clovers and the vetches crowding the sheltered valley. What an incredible Creator God we have. Psalm 104:31 says, 'May the glory of the LORD endure forever; may the LORD rejoice in his works', and that day I was also rejoicing in his creation.

One of the joys of being a rural police officer was the ability to go and explore some of the beautiful countryside that formed my beat, familiarising myself with the more 'off-the-beaten-track' places I may have been called to find one day.

When I was stationed at Stamford Bridge, as well as being responsible for the village itself, I looked after 200 square miles which included the amazing countryside that rises from the Vale of York, with its hills, charming hidden villages, and some of the wild and distinctive dry chalk valleys of the Yorkshire Wolds.

Many of these villages are truly remote and remain almost unchanged by the modern world; some of them have quaint, romantic names like Hanging Grimston, Bugthorpe and Uncleby. These picturesque hamlets were scattered throughout the steep-sided green valleys with dry stone walls where sheep and cattle often roamed free and made their own white tracks across the fields. There would usually be a few cottages made from pale, limestone blocks, often with brightly coloured doors, a few flowers around and washing hanging out to dry. Tiny, ancient stone churches could be found and the occasional old pub nestled itself among the houses. This is an area of idyllic scenery and yet it remains so unknown to the outside world. Not many outsiders frequent the Wolds, apart from long-distance walkers on the Wolds Way or the age-old Roman roads, the dedicated ornithologists seeking rare birds, or those botanists hunting the abundant wildflowers unique to the environment. My area included Millington Pastures and Millington Wood – a designated area of special scientific interest.

Every three years shotgun certificates needed to be renewed, forcing me to visit gunowners to identify the guns and check that the security arrangements were adequate. Normally, they should be kept in a locked gun cabinet. If someone owned a Section 1 firearm, such as a rifle for shooting deer, the arrangements were far stricter; I even had to count how much ammunition they had compared to what they'd purchased. Often, older men working on these isolated farms alone lived in primitive conditions. Sometimes an offer that sounded nice, like, 'Do you wanna cuppa, lad?' resulted in a cup of over-sweetened tea served in a dirty jam jar. I soon learnt to search out a hard chair to avoid any tiny six-legged creatures lurking in the soft furnishings. Early in my career on a rural beat I inadvertently took home such a creature, leading to several weeks of applying cream to a very tender part of my anatomy. Never again.

The unusual name of one village led to a rather strange request from a fellow PC. One day I got a phone call from a policeman in another force. His hobby was 'philately' – stamp collecting. He especially sort First Editions. A new set of stamps was being produced, celebrating the amazing insect life of the British Isles. He thought it would be great to have the First Edition stamped at the local post office in Bugthorpe, one of my villages, making them unique to collectors. I was only too happy to oblige.

Another advantage of being a rural bobby was I no longer had to work full night shifts. I only worked half-nights – 6 p.m. to 2 a.m. When I did that shift, especially on a weekend, I would usually double up with the Pocklington police car, so the two of us were available together. I would join them at about 10 p.m. so we could be double handed for the pub's closing time.

Pocklington boasted a posh grammar school, where the likes of William Wilberforce, famous for his involvement in the abolition of slavery, went to school. There was a constant rivalry between the grammar school and the local secondary school, which often erupted into acts of violence.

I remember one autumn when it seemed like every weekend I worked would end up with us arresting some of the teenage youths from Pocklington for minor criminal damage: a vandalised phone box, drunk and disorderly conduct, and screaming at police vehicles while blocking the roads. One youth, well known to the local police, seemed to be arrested most weeks. Whenever he had committed an offence, such as damaging a phone box, he would linger, as though he was waiting for the police to come and arrest him. Somehow, it was always me taking him in.

One highlight of life in Yorkshire during the autumn was Hull Fair, one of Europe's largest fairground events. When I was stationed in Hull it was always considered a good way to make some money; they were always looking for extra staff and they paid overtime so there was never a shortage of volunteers. Not to mention how much manpower was needed to sort out the fights. In the weeks leading up to Hull Fair, smaller fairs with rides, amusement stalls and food vendors would stop off at towns and villages on route. Every year one would set up in Pocklington. They would stay for a few nights on the green beside the grammar school, and this would usually lead to rivalries between different demographic groups.

So, it was a Friday night, a beautiful autumn evening and the fair had come to town. I was on half-nights and was expected to be in Pocklington earlier than usual to help to cover the fair. One of the psalms says that 'The LORD makes firm the steps of the one who delights in him' (Psalm 37:23). That day I was to find out the truth in that verse.

Knowing I would be busy later, I decided I'd spend the early part of my shift patrolling the smaller villages of the Wolds. At the bottom of Garrowby Hill there was a huge mansion called Garrowby Hall, owed by the late Queen's cousin, Lord Halifax. Nestled in the hills, high up on the Wolds, above the hall is The Dower House where his mother lived. I found myself driving in that general direction, where the roads peter out into farm tracks and gated roads. Gated roads are so called because you must stop the vehicle, open a gate, drive through it, stop again and then close the gate behind you.

In one of those beautiful, sheltered valleys, I decided to stop for a while. I pulled off at the side of the road where sheep were grazing peacefully in front of me. It was a glorious evening and I thought it would be a great opportunity to get some paperwork done. There were always plenty of shotgun applications to deal with. Probably because of the sheep on the hillsides, quietly cropping the lush green grass, I found myself thinking about David, the shepherd boy in the Bible. I felt so grateful for the wonderful place God had brought us to live. I began to think through some the verses of Psalm 23. 'He makes me lie down in green pastures, he leads me beside quiet waters, he restores my soul' (Psalm 23:2-3). Everything was so tranquil, still and peaceful.

After a couple of hours, it was time to be making my way back to Pocklington. I was surprised I hadn't heard anything on the radio. I drove back up the road through the gate and up the hill and suddenly the radio burst into life. They were repeatedly shouting my call sign, 'Charlie Romeo fifty-five, come in. Charlie Romeo fifty-five!'

Charlie: C division, Romeo: Rural officer and my radio number – fifty-five.

They had been desperately trying to get hold of me to say I shouldn't go to Pocklington. The Lord, whom I had been meditating on as 'my Shepherd', clearly knew Pocklington was a bad idea that night; I believe he led me to those green pastures up on the Wolds for my protection.

That night, the youth I'd been consistently arresting had decided he was going to kill me. He was drunk again and I became the focus of all his life's failures – the cause of all his misery. He was once again facing a court case and it was all because of me. Having gone to his grandfather's house, he had stolen the shotgun out of the garage and gone to Pocklington fair where he knew I would be. He intended to ambush me and shoot me dead.

Instead of finding me he'd bumped into the local Pocklington PC, who he had held at gunpoint in the fair for about an hour. All that time he had been ranting and raving, 'Get Wilksie here.'

Back then, we didn't carry guns ourselves and firearms teams were few and far between. Today, a firearms team would arrive at any incident within fifteen minutes. For the last hour, my colleagues had been trying to warn me not to go to Pocklington. God had already taken me to a radio blind spot. Once it was obvious to the youth I wasn't coming, he didn't shoot the PC but in frustration, turned the gun on himself and permanently injured himself.

This was one of many occasions where I have known God saved me from serious harm. I wouldn't normally have been out on the hills that day, I merely felt his prompting to go there. And when I get to heaven, I'm sure I'll realise how many times he's protected me without me even knowing.

Chapter Five

Injured in the Line of Duty

Every Thursday was court day at Pocklington. The police station had two cells, and adjacent to it was the beautiful, ornate Magistrates' Court. Three magistrates held court each week, and they mainly dealt with traffic offences, but occasionally, there were public order cases and minor property damages to attend to. Anything more complicated was referred to York Crown Court.

On the borders of Pocklington, there was a secure children's home where criminal offenders were housed if they were too young to be sent to Borstal. For the last three or four weeks, two youths had been brought before the magistrates every week. They were on remand to the secure unit until their case came before the Crown Court. They had to appear in court every week while they waited for their case to progress. Afterwards, they were returned to the cells until their escorts picked them up later in the day.

Over the weeks, we began to know the kids well; they were polite, well-behaved and didn't cause us many problems. We rather liked them. So much so we included them in our fish and chips lunch each week, instead of giving them the frozen ready meals prisoners usually received. I had been part of the team each Thursday and it was just another routine court day. The two young criminals were escorted into court to stand before the magistrates. We stood either side of them when the prosecuting solicitor had asked for a further remand in custody; there were no objections and the magistrates had agreed to it for another week.

As I turned to lead the boys out, one of them punched me in the mouth, knocking me to the floor before making a run for it. His friend stood there, horrified. Apparently, they had planned to escape together but he chickened out at the last minute.

So, there I was, lying on the floor. The magistrates decided it was time for a cup of tea, leaving me completely stunned, totally helpless, dazed and incapable of doing anything. The other PC grabbed the lad who had hit me and grappled with him, finally crashing through the panel of the glass door but continuing to hold firmly onto his prisoner. The boys were escorted back to the cells while I was helped through the adjoining door to the police station by other officers.

My lips were split and my blood was everywhere. They rang the doctor's surgery down the road and the doctor came straight away. I needed stitches and rather than giving me three injections to numb my mouth, he thought it would be easier to sew up the cuts without anaesthetic. To say it hurt would be an understatement.

It turned out the perpetrator had received a letter from his girlfriend, ending their relationship so he decided to run away. It was astonishing that this was the worst injury I'd sustained so far in service, especially considering all I'd been through: the fights, the Toxeth riots, the public order events, and the petrol bombs that had been thrown at me and the threats that had been made against me. And I was brought down by the most unexpected assailant. Unbeknown to me, he had martial arts training; he'd learnt how to throw a punch and to wait until his opponent was unprepared before instigating an attack.

When I arrived home, my young children took one look at me and ran away to hide. I was drinking through a straw for a couple of weeks, and sore for quite a long time, but at least I got some financial remuneration through the Criminal Injuries Board. But I still have the scars today.

Being a police officer is an inherently dangerous job, with PCs regularly being threatened, assaulted and sometimes killed. These are not always deliberate acts. Many are simply the result of people trying to escape. Through the years of their service, any PC doing their job properly will be injured on duty. In my case, the injuries were relatively minor, and I thank the Lord for his amazing protection.

It was a late summer's evening. I was out on patrol in my shirtsleeves, it was that warm. I was accompanied by a Special Constable called Stan. Special Constables were members of the public who chose to work alongside the police in a voluntary capacity but they still wore police uniform and had similar powers to us.

Stan was six-foot tall with a drinker's belly, a round smiling face and a heart of gold. By day he was a farm labourer, but he chose to partner with me at night; he wouldn't go out with anyone else. He was as strong as an ox and not someone to mess with; I remember him dangling an aggressive youth over the bridge in Stamford Bridge on one occasion. The youth and his mates proved to be no further problem to us after Stan join us.

So, on that summer's evening, at 11.30 p.m. Stan and I received a radio call to go to the village of Allerthorpe where a ten-year-old girl had gone missing. She had been out playing with a friend and hadn't returned home. Her parents, understandably, were distraught.

Allerthorpe is a small village close to Pocklington but is separated from the town by the busy A1079 from Hull to York. We joined a large group of officers who had responded to the call; there were two dog handlers, an inspector, a couple of sergeants, two traffic officers and anyone else who wasn't busy that night. The traffic officers had come mainly because Allerthorpe was next to the main road, making an abduction quite possible, or for her to be at the mercy of the traffic.

We met on the outskirts of Allerthorpe and were to conduct a search of the farms, barns and other outbuildings in the area. Her friend had given some information about the last barn the girl was seen in and before we even started searching, one of the dog handlers found her fast asleep in there. There was much rejoicing, especially by her parents.

But that was when the trouble started. Like most small villages, there was a pub in Allerthorpe. In those days, village pubs were supposed to stop serving alcohol by 11 p.m. By now, it was half-past twelve and we were getting ready to head back to our own areas. However, the village pub's lights were still on, the carpark was full, and the sound of merrymaking permeated the summer night. Unfortunately, this was one of my villages and the inspector was not happy. He couldn't turn a blind eye, especially when he had sufficient staff around to deal with it. It was time to shut the pub down. He marched in with a sergeant and a couple of other officers shouting, 'Empty this pub straight away.'

Forty or fifty drunken men and women emerged from the pub, faced with a veritable army of police officers waiting for them. Living their rural lives, they'd probably never seen anything like it; police cars of all shapes and sizes lined the road.

I have learnt over the years that warm summer nights and alcohol never mix well. If this happened during the winter, the crowd would have wandered home to shelter from the cold.

Instead, they hung around outside the pub, boisterous and loud, and it was not very long before they started shouting abuse at us. Then someone threw a bottle. And so, we were forced to disperse them. Stan and I started to herd a couple of locals up the road away from the pub. They didn't like that. Starting to kick down neighbours' fences as they went, we had no choice but to arrest them, especially when the inspector was there. As we neared one of their own homes, we attempted to restrain and arrest them but one of them did something about it.

To this day, I can't recall the exact sequence of events. Out of the corner of my eye, I saw him pick something up off the ground. At first, I thought it was a large stick as he began to swing it at my head. Somehow, instead of hitting my head, the weapon connected squarely with my back and hit my shoulder blade with great force. It felt to me as though I had been pushed out of harm's way, but it couldn't have been Stan because he had been struggling with the other man. Afterwards, I discovered that the weapon was one half of a pair of children's stilts. It was four-foot long, wooden, and reinforced with large, steel bolts that attached the footplate at right angles to the main pole. If it had hit my head, it certainly could have been serious. Looking back, it seems miraculous; I was only in my shirtsleeves and yet I didn't receive any injuries. I wasn't even bruised, even though the stilt broke into three pieces.

Rather than being arrested for criminal damage, that man was arrested for assaulting a police officer. His brother, who had been struggling with Stan, ran through the house, out the back door and across the fields. He was later arrested for being drunk and disorderly. A few weeks later, it was hard to explain the whole incident to a magistrate's court. How was it possible that I had been hit with such a strong child's stilt and yet had no visible marks? To give this further perspective, had it hit my head, I could have died or suffered severe brain damage.

Over the years I have experienced God's divine protection on several occasions. The Bible expresses this so clearly: 'The LORD is my light and my salvation – whom shall I fear? The LORD is the stronghold of my life – of whom shall I be afraid?' (Psalm 27:1)

Chapter Six

Reign of Terror

It was a beautiful morning in summer. The river was flowing swiftly, its surface dappled with sunlight as it ran beneath the bridge that carried the single-track road. This bridge was the boundary between our force in Humberside and North Yorkshire's police force. During the summer of 1982, North Yorkshire Police were in trouble.

They had called together twelve police forces from across the country to undertake the largest police manhunt there had ever been in Great Britain. However, the man they were hunting was also hunting them. Although his name was Barry Prudom, he had been nicknamed 'The Phantom in the Forest' because of his crimes. For the last two weeks they had been chasing him around the Malton area. Prudom had already killed several serving police officers, and now his reign of terror was to end.

Several days of heightened tension followed with a palpable sense of unease. I was warned that I needed to be extra vigilant on my routine calls that still needed to be made. Some of my villages were less than ten miles from Malton across country, but local farmers still required visits and shotgun enquiries had to be answered.

We knew that Prudom had been trained in the Territorial Army, gaining the much-coveted position as one of the fittest and well-trained soldiers in their SAS unit. He knew how to blend in with the countryside, how to create a 'hide' and live off the land for days or weeks at a time. A respected marksman and used to working alone, he depended entirely on his own skills to survive. It was believed that his hide was in Dalby Forest, but that was only conjecture. We knew he could be anywhere, but because so many extra police officers had been drafted into North Yorkshire to find him, there was an even greater chance he would slip across the border into my area.

Once again, my night shift was disturbed by a radio call. Just after midnight the alarm at Garrowby Hall was triggered. Normally when that happened, which was every few months, I would be the only officer responding to the call. I would make my way to the huge sprawling mansion and set about checking the hall, the outbuildings and stables, the outdoor swimming pool, and the workers' cottages. Lord Halifax was the late Queen's cousin and there were many valuable antiques and paintings held there.

That night was totally different. I was alone in my car, but every other police car in the area was there too, including a firearms team from Hull. Lord Halifax was certainly surprised to see so many of us. The senior officer went into the house with him to search while we formed a cordon around the buildings.

Garrowby is a huge estate set in a dip in the hills. It's the middle of nowhere, with no streetlights. That night, there was hardly any moonlight and it was difficult to even see the officer next to you in line. Although we had torches, their light didn't pick up much detail and, in the days before high visibility coats, we were all in black with no flashes on our jackets or anything that would make us easier targets for Prudom. I remember a particular dog handler; his large, viscous Alsatian barking and growling added to the tension as we pensively waited. Prudom would not be easy to arrest and it was likely he could try to shoot his way out of the situation.

Eventually, the inspector returned to tell us it had been a false alarm. We were to continue with our usual duties but would remain extra vigilant.

The next morning, I was called to the Pocklington Police Station for a briefing with all the other officers in the area. We were to man the bridge at Stamford Bridge and stop and search every vehicle coming from North Yorkshire. Malton was Prudom's last known location and was only a mere twelve miles away. My team for the task was myself and my sergeant. I was so pleased that he was firearms trained, until they told us that all firearms had been committed elsewhere. They did provide us with a consolation prize – body armour. These weren't like modern Kevlar jackets but were leftovers from the Second World War. The jackets were made from steel plates stuffed inside hessian sacking; they were heavy, but they would stop a bullet.

Between us and Malton, there was just a few miles of open countryside, providing perfect hiding places for a killer who had been trained by the SAS. And so, my sergeant and I were standing on the Humberside end of the bridge that morning. The first car came over the bridge and Sarge put up his hand to stop the vehicle. We looked inside the seats and then asked the driver to open the boot. I must say that my heart was in my mouth, my throat was dry, and I was sweating under the hessian jacket. I had never done anything like this before. Police work is 70 per cent boredom and 30 per cent excitement, fear and tension. This was the next level.

That morning, we were probably both thinking about the dog-handler Prudom had killed a few days earlier. He had shot the policeman seven times, before shooting his dog, which had tried to defend him. This had happened a few miles away in the local beauty spot of Dalby Forest. Prudom had then made his escape into the surrounding woodlands.

We stood either side of the car as the boot slowly opened, revealing a couple of cardboard boxes and a shopping bag. Relief flooded through me as we thanked the driver and invited him to move along. Then we started the whole process again with the next vehicle. It was going to be a long morning.

The traffic on the bridge was controlled by lights. By the time we had stopped three cars, the lights changed and allowed vehicles from Humberside to cross into North Yorkshire. This meant we had a short respite from the tension. During this time, we happened to see an old man using the footpath from the far side of the bridge. He was wearing a scruffy, long coat and walked straight to us. As he approached, he dug his hand into his pocket.

'Here, lads,' he said, 'I know what you are doing.'

He then produced an oily rag from the pocket and handed it to my sergeant. Sarge opened it to find a Second World War Smith and Wesson revolver, in pristine condition and fully loaded. Never mind the legality of the situation, we were not going to refuse his gift when it helped us to feel safe. As the next car came over the bridge, he ambled back the way he had come.

Putting his firearms training into practice, from then on Sarge pointed the gun at the boot while I opened it with him covering me. The job seemed far less scary than before. We were there for several hours and searched many vehicles. That afternoon, the siege of Malton began to wind down and a fully equipped firearms team came to relieve us. Just before they arrived, we looked up and saw the elderly gentleman walk back across the bridge. Sarge carefully wrapped the gun up in its oily rag and returned it to him. As another car appeared, we didn't see the man leave nor did we see where he went. We never told a single person about that gun.

Eventually Prudom was caught and killed in an exchange of gunfire with armed police. Sarge felt that perhaps it would be good to get the gun out of circulation, as it was most likely an illegally held firearm. As the rural bobby living in Stamford Bridge, the job fell to me. I knew most people from the Humberside end of the bridge and was reasonably familiar with a few folks on the other side. In 1982, on the North Yorkshire side of Stamford Bridge, there was only a handful of houses, a garage, a factory, and a pub. Despite visiting every house to make enquiries, no one knew anyone who fit my description of the old man. I never found him.

I have often thought about that scary time. It's safe to say we both had a greater confidence and sense of peace in fulfilling our duty after we got the revolver. A beautiful verse in the book of psalms says, 'The angel of the LORD encamps around those who fear him, and he delivers them' (Psalm 34:7).

Chapter Seven

The Many Faces of Death

My breath came out in clouds of white vapour as my icy fingers fumbled to open the door of the tiny caravan. I knew what to expect, but the scene before me was still disturbing and bizarre.

A young man knelt at the side of his bed, his body stiff now, either with rigor mortis or through the freezing air in the van. His head was resting on the counterpane, alongside several small piles of money. Was this a robbery gone wrong? But why would they leave the cash? Who had killed him, and why? With these questions still buzzing around my head, I fulfilled my responsibility to call in the necessary authorities as the first one on the scene.

In the late 1980s, during my posting at Stamford Bridge, a new high-security prison was being built at Full Sutton. This was to be a high-security unit within a prison and took several years to build and therefore needed a large workforce to build it. Some of these workers lived in caravans on site. One cold Saturday morning I received a call to attend the prison site because a body had been found. Crunching across the frozen ground, trying hard to avoid the iced puddles, I was shown to a small, dirty caravan. The deceased was a fit young man in his twenties. I found him knelt on the floor by the bed with his head resting on the bedcovers.

As the incident happened on the prison site their Health and Safety Executive was there, and although it was being treated as an industrial accident, it attracted a greater level of scrutiny than usual. We waited in the cold for the doctor to arrive and validate the death before a 'scenes of crime' photographer was called, along with the forensic pathologist, before finally, after almost a full day, I had to wait for the undertaker. During the day, I was putting together the scenes of crime log, filling in the details of every attendant to the scene.

As the day wore on, I had good suspicions over his death and once the pathologist arrived, they knew immediately that the young man had died of carbon monoxide poisoning. The people who discovered the body had found the gas burners turned on and had switched them off.

I attended the coroner's inquest about a year later where I met the family of the deceased. The inquest brought in a verdict of death by misadventure. Having returned from work on the Friday night with his wages, it seemed the young man had lit the gas burners to keep himself warm, as there was no central heating in the van. He knelt on the floor to count his money, and he wouldn't have smelt anything but would have felt tired and dropped off to sleep. The caravan was old and poorly ventilated with no windows open; the oxygen in the small amount of fresh air would have produced carbon dioxide. However, the gas burners then continued to use the gradually reducing amount of oxygen to produce carbon monoxide, a very poisonous gas, which, unfortunately, the human body preferentially absorbs over oxygen. It kills very quickly.

After witnessing its distressing effect for myself, I am very particular about having carbon monoxide monitors in my home and have them regularly checked.

A serving police officer sees more death than is probably good for them. Whenever somebody dies, and the doctor cannot immediately issue a death certificate, the police are called to investigate the circumstances around the death to produce a report for the coroner. Unlike on American television shows, here in England the coroner doesn't attend the scene – the police do. If the attending PC feels there is anything suspicious about the death, they escalate the investigation to the CID (Criminal Investigation Department), and the pathologist may get involved.

I lost track of how many times I was called to the scene of a dead body. It was, perhaps, as many as one every couple of months. In most cases, these sudden deaths are not suspicious. With the usual process, a doctor will be called to validate the death at the scene before a body can be moved. Once the doctor is satisfied the death isn't suspicious, an undertaker will be called, and the body will be taken to the undertaker's Chapel of Rest. If the doctor cannot issue a death certificate, the undertaker will still be called but the body will be taken to the hospital mortuary to await a post-mortem. The police would accompany the body to the mortuary, and would often be involved in stripping the body, putting it in refrigeration and bagging up the clothes. This would especially be the case at night when no mortuary attendants were available. If an ambulance had been called because the person was unwell, they would occasionally transport the body to the hospital mortuary and the police would follow to preserve the continuity of evidence. The PC's job was then to complete the paperwork, including a statement of identification from a loved one. The file would also need to record the circumstances of the death, including what the person's last meal had been, what medication they were on, their GP details and the circumstances of how the body was found.

After the post-mortem, the findings would be added to the file, which would then be sent to a coroner's office. An inquest would determine the cause of death, be it by misadventure, accident, murder, unlawful killing, or suicide. Throughout my service I have attended every conceivable style of death, from road traffic accidents to murder scenes and accidental deaths at home and in workplaces.

Most of these deaths have been sad, some bizarre, and some, dare I say, funny; sometimes, the most difficult of situations can have an element of humour in them. There is a certain black humour policemen develop to cope with the things they see.

One evening, myself and my special constable, Stan, were called to a house in Stamford Bridge where a retired police constable had died. We were met at the front door by his wife, who I knew. She took us upstairs to where her husband had died, while he was having a bath. Death was not unexpected, as he had been having several heart issues. His wife took it in her stride. I think being married to a policeman helped her in this situation. Still in the bath, he was a large man and his body almost filled the tub. His wife had pulled the plug and carefully placed a face flannel over his private parts.

A doctor was able to issue a death certificate, so his wife decided to call one of the local undertakers to remove the body. We waited with her until he arrived. Unfortunately for us, she had chosen one of the less professional firms, run by an elderly man and a small team of assistants. When the van arrived, it seemed the elderly owner had unfortunately come alone. To make matters worse, when he arrived he took me to one side and sheepishly explained he could hardly walk because he had put a nail through his foot. He almost pleaded with us to help him with the body. That was not our job.

He had a chat with the wife before shutting her in the front room and crawling up the stairs on his hands and knees. So, we were forced to help him. Picture the scene as the three of us manhandled a large man, still wet and slippery, out of the bath and into the undertaker's wide rubber body-bag. We then dragged the body across the landing and down the stairs, which was not an easy task. This was made harder because the stairs had a half-landing, and as the undertaker was crawling down backwards, he managed to knock over and break a large ornamental vase. It was hard to keep a straight face.

Some unusual deaths are more distressing than others, especially when dealing sympathetically with those who have lost loved ones.

No wonder the police 'harden their hearts'. Generally, they are dealing with good people at difficult moments, or they deal with the worst of what people can do to each other. The constant nature of this can make you feel heartless, which is not a good place to be, but thank God that he is able to change people's hearts.

It's always tragic when somebody takes their own life. Over the years, I've come across several suicides. In many ways, it stems from a form of mental illness; people get to the point where they can't see another way out of a terrible situation, or they feel that their world, and everyone in it, would be better off without them. They seem unable to comprehend that their loved ones must carry on without them, picking up the pieces and trying to come to terms with the way they died.

Early one spring afternoon I received a radio message to attend one of the smaller villages on my patch. A husband had failed to return home the previous night. He was a builder and was in the process of building a new house for his family and had been spending every spare moment there. The visit may have been considered a 'welfare check', as he was working alone and could have been in an accident.

I arrived at the building site to see the makings of a lovely, detached house with a pick-up parked in the driveway. The front doorway was open; there was no door, only a board propped up at the entrance. I knocked and announced myself but the place was eerily quiet. I let myself in and proceeded to search each room. There were tools around the place and an empty coffee cup sat on a windowsill but the kettle was cold. I did a thorough search of the ground floor before climbing the staircase to find all the doorways open but one. I assumed it was the bathroom. After knocking and getting no response, I tried the door. It was locked, so I started to force it open. This is never an easy decision to make as any unnecessary damage a PC causes is paid for by the police. Contrary to most television shows, gaining entry through a locked door never works by hitting the door with your shoulder. It would cause bruising at the very least, possibly dislocating the shoulder, or perhaps injuring your neck. The way to gain entry is by the size-ten key — one swift kick at the door in line with the lock. So, I took one step away from the door and then threw all my body weight behind a straight legged kick. Not many doors can withstand such a kick with a seventeen-stone guy behind it.

This door gave way easily enough. I found the man in a position I had never come across before. He was laid on the floor with a leather jacket over his head, secured by a belt tied around his neck, and his wrists were hand-cuffed behind his back. He was clearly dead. Initially, it looked like he'd been the subject of an assassination. I immediately called for 'scenes of crime officers' (SOCOs), a doctor, and the CID – we needed the entire circus.

There was no outward sign of any trauma and gradually the suspicion of murder was replaced with the certainty he had taken his own life. For one thing, the key was still in the door and had been locked from the inside. It could have felt like one of those Sherlock Holmes 'locked room' mysteries but in the end, it proved to be suicide. Drowning under mounting debt and fearing financial ruin, the man suffocated himself using the coat and belt. He then handcuffed his hands behind his back so he couldn't change his mind.

The thing was, I felt nothing after this incident, just like when I saw an old lady's body.

Alzheimer's is a terrible disease. It not only robs people of their memories but it also takes away their ability to make decisions for themselves. While we were at Stamford Bridge, we were part of a close-knit village community. Our children went to the local school and play group. Ann taught piano to a few local children. In one of the local homes, an elderly resident had Alzheimer's. Sometimes she would disappear and walk around the neighbourhood alone. On several occasions, I'd be involved in finding her wandering around the area and returning her to the home.

Being a small village, everyone knew this woman. So, when one spring morning she went missing again, everyone was keeping an eye out. This time, clothes were found below the bridge where fishermen cast their lines into the fast-flowing River Derwent. I recovered the clothes and spoke to the home. They belonged to the missing resident. I completed a missing person's report on her and, due to her illness, we were not expecting to find her alive. It appeared as if she ended up in the river. In a small village, news soon spreads. It was a difficult time.

Three days passed. Unbeknown to me, a group of local people had decided to continue searching the riverbanks with high hopes. It was a warm, mild Sunday afternoon and I was enjoying some family time while I was off duty. There was a knock at our door and a member of the public, who had been walking his dog, told me he had found the body. My day off ended abruptly as I rang Pocklington Police Station.

The inspector answered the phone and decided he would take charge himself. He told me to wait for him to arrive and when he did, we joined the walker and his dog and set off down the riverbank path from the bridge for one and a half miles. At last, the man indicated something close to the bank. To me, whatever it was looked like a small grey-brown circular mat. It proved to be the top of her head so close to the bank edge that it was almost covered by the overhanging vegetation.

The inspector decided we should get the body out of the river. It was a struggle as we splashed around in the muddy water, slipping and sliding among the water weeds and wild plants. Eventually, we managed to get hold of the body and manoeuvre it out of the water and onto the path.

The inspector called a local undertaker to meet us. As the inspector was somewhat familiar with the area, he decided the best place for the undertaker to meet us would be in a lay-by on the A166. This meant we had to carry the body another one and a half miles in the opposite direction through fields, across fences and hedges, and finally into a wooded area next to the road. It was so awful. The memory of the three of us manhandling and carrying this poor, dead, dripping, partially dressed, frail elderly lady isn't a pleasant one. Unlike the body of the retired police officer, this poor lady didn't have the dignifying cover of an undertaker's black body carrier.

Early in my career, I strongly believed that I needed to toughen up and so indulged in many of a policeman's coping mechanisms such as black humour, teasing, and the culture of heavy drinking. However, there's always the danger of becoming so hardened that it's easy not to care for the public, colleagues and even family. God says, 'I will remove from you your heart of stone and give you a heart of flesh' (Ezekiel 36:26). In Matthew's Gospel, Jesus quotes the Old Testament and says, 'For this people's heart has become calloused; they hardly hear with their ears, and they have closed their eyes. Otherwise they might see with their eyes, hear with their ears, understand with their hearts and turn, and I would heal them' (Matthew 13:15).

And I needed my heart changing.

Chapter Eight

Heart of Stone

A couple of years after we moved to Stamford Bridge, in around 1983, a few close events showed how much my heart had turned to stone.

Christmas is always a fascinating time for the police. We were often on stand-by and working from our offices on Christmas Day, which was usually quiet. Boxing Day was entirely the opposite. It wasn't uncommon to deal with a domestic on Boxing Day as families fell out about expected presents which didn't materialise and pubs were open at lunchtime. Mixing drink with disappointment was a recipe for disaster.

We had been at Stamford Bridge for a couple of years and I was working on Boxing Day. I was about to leave for my Boxing Day family lunch when I got a radio message about an accident at Kexby on the A1079. The A1079 crosses the River Ouse on a road bridge at Kexby which is the boundary between the Humberside and North Yorkshire police forces. The accident was in the middle of the bridge. When I arrived at the scene, there was a traffic car from North Yorkshire and an ambulance in attendance. Two cars had been involved in a head-on collision, leaving one car on the North Yorkshire side of the bridge and one on our side. The North Yorkshire's traffic cop was dealing with the driver at his side, so naturally I went to deal with the other car.

It was a small, silver sports car with extensive front-end damage. The driver was still in the car; she was in her early thirties, dressed in expensive riding jodhpurs and a tweed jacket. She was conscious so I got into the passenger seat beside her to wait for another ambulance and the fire brigade to cut her out. I remember trying to keep her calm, assuring her that everything would be OK. She told me she had just been riding at her stables but was in a lot of pain and had obviously been drinking. I sat talking to her for what felt like ages. Eventually, the ambulance and fire brigade arrived to force the door open. I helped the crew lift her out of the car and onto a stretcher. It was while I was still holding her hand that she died. I certainly wasn't expecting it.

At a road traffic accident, the traffic officer does all the paperwork. The traffic officer from North Yorkshire said he would deal with it, which left me to follow the ambulance in my panda car to the mortuary at York District Hospital. There is a particular smell about a mortuary, a strong scent of carbolic soap. To this day, that smell can transport me back to those images. There was a mortuary attendant available so I helped to undress the victim, cut the boots from her damaged legs, and bag up her clothes, in case they were needed for forensic examination. I itemised all her belongings, put a label on her big toe, and helped to put her body in the fridge. There is such a sense of finality as the metal drawer clangs shut.

That was the end of my involvement with the case. I went home from the hospital for my belated Boxing Day lunch. As it was part of the job, I filed it away in my head. I don't think I even talked to Ann about it until some time had passed.

Of all the deaths police officers attend, the death of a child is potentially the most distressing. Two or three months after the incident at Kexby, I received a call to attend the scene of a cot death. I thought the address sounded familiar; it turned out that it was the old police house at Wilberfoss. When I arrived, an ambulance had already arrived along with the local doctor and, of course, the distressed parents. I was informed the doctor had pronounced the baby dead and because of the circumstances, the ambulance would take the body to Hull. My job was to take some notes of the scene and complete the paperwork.

I entered the house we had once called home and ascended the familiar staircase to the child's bedroom. I opened the same door where my baby boy had once slept to find the wallpaper I had put up. There was a cot exactly where our baby's cot used to stand and there inside it was the tiny body of a dead baby. And I felt nothing.

I completed the paperwork and went home.

'Just another day at the office!'

At times, God must do some serious surgery within us to create the man or woman he can use in the future. A couple of weeks later, the penny dropped and I realised that I should have been devastated by these two deaths. I'd shrugged them off and hidden behind the wall I created to protect my emotions. It had worked well but it also stopped me from expressing emotional happiness or love. I knew if I was going to be a good policeman, and an even better husband and father, this wall had to come down. So one quiet afternoon in my office, with paperwork strewn across my desk, I cried out to God to do something before it was too late.

The Bible recounts when impregnable walls came tumbling down as God stepped into a situation. The fortified city of Jericho stood in the way of the Israelites' conquest of the promised land. Jericho citizens had heard about God miraculously leading the Israelites out of Egypt and keeping them safe through years of wandering in the desert, but the people of Jericho still felt that they were all safe behind their walls.

They continued to trust in the walls even when the Israelites began to silently walk around their city for six days. Then on the seventh day, the Israelites walked around the city six more times. I imagine that's when Jericho's people started to get nervous. Finally, on the seventh time around, trumpets blasted loudly, rending the air, and all the Israelites shouted for victory. That was the moment the walls fell (Joshua 6).

As I was writing the starting drafts of this book, it just so happened that a personal friend of ours, Kezia, shared her thoughts on this story with us and it resonated deeply with me:

At this point, the people captured the city. God wants to do the same thing with our hearts. Brick by brick He wants to break down the surrounding walls of our hearts. This was an occasion to be celebrated as the thing that they had been pursuing for a week resulted in a massive victory! God is pursuing you in the same way and He won't stop! His pursuit of you is because He wants your heart and your life. He has great plans for us and when we allow Him to pursue us, those walls can begin to come down and He can come into our hearts and transformation can happen.[1]

I asked the Lord to step into my situation and he did. A few weeks later, I attended another sudden death. As I was talking

---

1. Kezia Jasmine, *Seeking Truth: 29 Days in God's Word* (Independently Published, 2023), Day 9

to the distraught widow, I realised I was struggling not to burst into tears myself. God had replaced my heart of stone with a heart of flesh. Over the following years, I worked hard not to build those hardened walls again, which allowed me to remain compassionate in tragic situations.

As we put pen to paper to share these stories, it just so happened that yesterday I was standing in a local car park when a family friend, who had just lost her mum, came over to me for a hug and we wept together over her loss. Men aren't called to be strong and silent types but are commanded to display the compassion, love and care we see in Jesus – the one we follow.

Chapter Nine

Romance is Not Dead

I had made such extra careful plans, but somehow everything was going wrong.

Ann and I had just gone through a pretty tough time. Work had taken over as number one in my life, again. I knew Ann was struggling with it when she wanted to go and have a chat with one of the older ladies at church. When she came back, I noticed a difference in her; she would put her arms around me as we watched the kids play or stroke my shoulder when she passed my chair on her way to put the kettle on. They were just little things but it showed a welcome change in her heart.

I mentioned it to her, and she confessed she was so disappointed with our marriage that she wondered if she loved me anymore. Work had become the most important thing in my life and she felt like she was bringing the children up alone and she was the only one interested in church. I was shocked. I hadn't even realised what was happening but looking back it's no surprise she'd felt like that.

'So, what changed?' I asked.

She told me the elder's wife had shared about how she'd gone through something similar. The wife followed some advice to do little things as though she still loved her husband and then ask God to reignite her love for him. The two women had prayed together and Ann too followed that advice. I had noticed but what surprised her the most was how well it worked. She now felt like she loved me more than she had for years.

I was amazed and so decided to plan something special. I wanted her to know I appreciated what she had done and that I loved her too. She really was my number one. It was nearly our seventh wedding anniversary and there was a joke going around at work about guys who got the 'seven-year itch'. I wanted our seventh anniversary to be the exact opposite. It would be a rekindling of our love for each other.

My plan was for my mum and dad to have Philip and Rachel for the night. They often had them during the day but I secretly packed them an overnight bag without Ann knowing. We dropped the kids off in the morning before heading towards the North York Moors, one of our favourite picnic places. Ann thought we were going for the day. I remember she packed homemade tandoori chicken, salad and a cheesecake.

The closer we drove to the moors, the darker the clouds became. Ann suggested we just head for home but I was not having my plans spoilt by a little rain. However, by the time we pulled off near one of our usual picnic spots, torrential rain was pouring down. We opted for a picnic in the car, not quite so romantic, but hey, the food was lovely.

Then came the first disaster. We had brought Sheba, our dog, who was always as good as gold on the moors. Unfortunately, lightning torched the skies, and thunder roared over the rugged landscape just as I put the picnic basket back in the boot. Sheba made a run from the car without waiting for her lead. In a quick moment, our well-behaved dog was tearing across the open moorland, scattering frightened sheep in her wake. Well, there was nothing for it – we had to pull on our non-waterproof coats and race after her. When we finally had her back on the lead, all three of us were thoroughly wet through. Now what? Sitting in the car with the rain teeming down, I turned the engine on to warm us up but we were soon surrounded with that familiar wet-dog smell. It wasn't the most romantic setting. I wondered about finding a coffee shop, but there out in the wilds, where would the best place be? Ann opened the map book but as I began to pull back onto the road, the car made an awful noise. So, we ended up looking for a village with a garage as well as a tea shop. After driving around, down those narrow lanes, we eventually found the tiniest petrol station with a lovely old chap who offered to sort it for us and it would be ready in a few hours. The rain had eased off and he recommended a craft shop that served coffee half a mile down the hill.

We took Sheba, pulled on our damp coats and went off in search of a warm drink. It turned out to be a long half mile. However, when we found the place, they took pity on us and let Sheba in too. We had to rush down our drinks, so we had enough time to get back. As we walked up the steep gradient, it started to rain again. What a day!

With the car temporarily fixed, we headed off. Ann assumed we were on our way to pick the kids up, but when we pulled into the car park of The Lion on Blakey Ridge, I said my mum wouldn't mind if we were a bit late and suggested we had a meal. Rather reluctantly, she came to the bar with me but her face was a picture when I told the bar tender, 'Mr and Mrs Wilks, we have a room booked for the night.'

Things picked up then. They led us to one of the oldest rooms in the place, apologising for the fact there was no ensuite as they opened the door to the biggest bedroom we'd ever slept in. There was an enormous free-standing bath at one end with the fluffiest white towels draped over a chair – the best way to warm up after our wet, miserable day. We enjoyed dinner, bed and breakfast before enjoying a sun-kissed morning walk accompanied by the call of a curlew. Romance was not dead!

Chapter Ten

Garrowby

Just outside Stamford Bridge is Garrowby Hill.

Driving that road is not an experience one forgets quickly. It's a huge hill that rises from the Vale of York to the top of the Yorkshire Wolds. Due to its nature, it attracts frequent incidents which require a police presence.

At the bottom of the hill there is an escape 'run-off' for lorries if their brakes fail. On several occasions, a lorry has missed the escape lane and run into the field at the bottom near the turn off for Bishop Wilton. I have been called to such an incident twice when an HGV has ended up on its side in the middle of the field with its cargo strewn across the grass. The first time, a truck was transporting a load of piglets to market. It was like something in a film; there were baby pigs everywhere. Some were running loose in the road; some were in the field; others stuck in the hedgerow; some injured, and unfortunately, some little dead bodies, too. It was my job to control traffic while a recovery truck came for the lorry and, of course, the piglets needed to be herded back to safety. The whole thing took hours.

The driver was OK, although somewhat shaken. As he began to lose control, the sheer weight of the vehicle pulled him over, but the cab was so reinforced that he sustained no permanent injuries.

Thankfully, it was a fine day – I've had to do traffic duty there in freezing winter conditions. That day, we had to close off the whole hill so the lorry could be dragged from the field. Plus, with all those pigs running about, there could have easily been more accidents. Unfortunately, it forced vehicles to take a huge diversion as the local roads were no good for the heavy traffic that usually uses Garrowby Hill. Drivers, quite naturally, were irate about the inconvenience.

I have to say, though, it was quite funny watching the farm labourers chasing those cheeky little pigs. It reminded me of that expression: herding cats. Well, herding piglets is much the same, especially when most of them are terrified or injured.

The second incident on Garrowby Hill involved a lorry carrying packets of dried dates. So when the lorry was eventually recovered, we didn't need to catch any livestock. The dates were simply left on the field. Although, I took some home and had a go at making date wine. I can't say it was a success; I never tried making wine again. I guess you can't be good at everything.

It was a freezing cold day in late autumn. The sun was shining brightly but doing nothing to combat the wintery temperatures. The trees were boasting their final splashes of colour – glowing yellows, oranges, deep reds and browns. I was wearing my best leather-soled shoes. They were immaculate, so bulled that the sunlight reflected off them, but they had no grip. My feet weren't my only problem. I was cold. I had been told I couldn't wear my overcoat and instead of my black leather gloves, I was only allowed thin white ones.

One of the tiny hamlets on my beat was expecting an important visitor who had insisted she didn't want to see anyone except her personal protection officers and the local police officer during her visit. The rest of the team – dog handlers, firearms and special branch officers – would be deployed out of sight.

The inspector briefed me a few days earlier. I shouldn't let the side down, should be on my best behaviour, wear my best uniform and look the best I could. He made comment on the fact I wasn't normally the smartest officer under his command.

Her Majesty the Queen regularly visited her cousin, Lord Halifax, at Garrowby Hall. When she was on an official state visit, she would travel on the special royal train to York and then be chauffeured to Garrowby. We would all be aware and sometimes, special teams of officers would be drafted in. However, when it was only a private family visit, she would slip out of London and be driven up without any public awareness. If these private trips fell across the weekend, she would attend the local church service. As a devout Christian and Head of the Church of England, it was her duty and custom to attend.

The closest church to Garrowby Hall was All Saints, located in the tiny hamlet of Kirby Underdale. The small stone church which served the quiet parish doesn't seat more than a couple of dozen people and when the Queen visited, only those who regularly worshipped there were allowed to go. The rest of the village, and the 2011 census stated that only 125 people lived there, were encouraged to wait outside the building to greet her and Prince Philip as they were leaving.

Throughout the week preceding the visit, all the picket fences were given a fresh coat of paint and the churchyard looked immaculate, although clearing away the leaves was proving difficult with the time of year.

The short service of morning prayer was over, the doors to the church flew open, and Her Majesty and Prince Philip started to leave. I was standing outside, straightening up to attention to salute them. They walked past and smiled, saying a word or two to me, before greeting the villagers who thronged the lane. There are not many people who can say they've been to church with the Queen.

Sometimes we are faced with things we could never imagine.

Red, bloodshot eyes stared straight at me. His head dropped low on his shoulders as he tried to make up his mind: should he attack me or continue to damage the property? His great shoulders rippled as he flexed his muscles beneath his glowing tan coat. Steam snorted from his flared nostrils as his right foreleg began to bury his hoofs into the ground with such a force that he dug furrows in the grass verge. A few yards away, a tractor lay in the hedge bottom with the farmer struggling to get free. I knew we needed the animal off the road and into the field, but what was going to persuade a two-ton bull to do that?

It had started out as an ordinary day. I'd been called out to what I thought was a simple traffic incident. Instead, I found a trailer by the side of the road with the door open and a tractor on its side. The two-ton bull often travelled this way when he was taken to neighbouring farms to impregnate their cows. He didn't know that on this day, he was headed for the slaughterhouse. I arrived at the roadside soon after he had managed to escape from the trailer and hurt himself in the act. I then found myself in the predicament of a stand-off with an angry bull while the traffic on the narrow country lane came to a complete standstill. He was so angry; he had charged at the tractor repeatedly until it finally flipped over.

Each time cars came close, the bull would charge at them. Soon after I arrived, another farmer brought his tractor to try and help but the bull just charged at that one too. We ended up putting a cordon around the area to keep traffic away from the danger.

I wasn't the only one called to do something out of my comfort zone that day. By mid-afternoon, the control room had decided to send a firearms team to put the bull down. These guys were simply armed traffic cops. In their arsenal, they carried solid pellets to be fired from a shotgun which were used to stop cars, when necessary. A solid shotgun pellet is a single lump of lead that would be fired into the engine block. Their best thought was to shoot the bull in the head.

As they were discussing this idea, the problems became obvious. A vet was to tranquilise the bull but he couldn't get near it and subsequently advised the team that to kill it, they would need to get extremely close to the angry animal. A shot from distance could just bounce off the heavy bones of the bull's forehead, and it was imperative that they killed the bull first time. Otherwise, they risked angering it even more. It didn't take long for them to decide it wasn't a good idea to try.

Eventually the problem was solved the good old-fashioned way. An elderly farmer, wise in the countryside way of the world, wandered up to the group in the field.

'Hang on there, lads,' he said, 'I'll be back in a minute.'

It wasn't long before he returned, gently leading a heifer with him. The bull took one look at the cow and shook his head, which caused spittle to fly around his jowls; he licked his lips and then meekly followed her back into the transporter. A long day had a happy ending, but perhaps not one the bull expected.

Experience is valuable. That's what the older farmer had, and it was worth sharing. The same is true in Christian circles.

Getting alongside someone who has experience is a great thing to do. I have always wanted to come alongside others who 'do' so I could learn some of their skills. I have had, and still do have, mentors whose advice I follow. I am still learning from them in the same way that I am a mentor to others. We are never too old to learn.

Later in my career as a detective, I was a tutor constable who trained other detectives. Today, I help to train preachers, evangelists and church leaders. That journey began one quiet Wednesday morning in September 1988.

The sunlight glinted through the beautiful stained-glass windows as I slowly made my way across the church to the Lady Chapel, where a few parishioners gathered for the early morning communion service. Ann had been attending regularly, and when my shifts allowed it, I reluctantly joined her and the children on a Sunday morning. However, this was the first time I had attended the midweek service. I quietly slipped into one of the back pews.

While policing, I realised that police life was very different from the lives other Christians lived. Policemen work hard, live hard and play hard. It's like being in an exclusive club; if you're not in the club, it's difficult to explain why it's so different from ordinary life. In the police, I was surrounded by the worst of humanity.

When we moved back to Driffield in 1988, I felt like a spiritual schizophrenic. On Sunday I was a godly man, but the rest of the week I was 'one of the boys.' It was as though I changed hats every other day. It was mentally exhausting.

So, on that quiet Wednesday morning, after the communion service had finished, Reverend Mark Simons stayed behind to ask me how I was. I found myself being honest about how difficult things had become. He said it was fine to be all those things at once – Christian and policeman. Looking back, it seemed such an obvious thing to say, but at the time it was inspirational. It was almost as if each time I put on my uniform, I had been Superman, coming out of the phone box, transformed from the average Clark Kent. Now, I felt free. I could just be me, and all these things were just facets of who I was: policeman, husband, father, friend, Christian.

Several months later, on another Wednesday morning in the same place, I felt God asking me if I'd be willing to leave the police and serve him in full-time ministry. We had two young children at the time and so after much discussion and prayer, Ann and I knew we would have to say 'yes' to the Lord. Yet a month later during the Wednesday morning service, I felt God say, just as clearly, that he wanted our hearts to be willing but the timing was not right. A seed was sown. I had always known he would lead me out of the police and into the next part of his plan.

But shortly after that, my career developed. I was promoted into the CID and started training to be involved in major incidents. A fresh wave of trouble was tumbling my way.

PART THREE

The Breaking

Chapter Eleven

Car Trouble

'They are all OK, just don't get mad,' shouted the inspector as he walked across the school car park towards me.

OK? Get mad? What was he talking about? He had radioed me to meet him at the school and then, I saw it. My pride and joy sat a few metres away. The best and most expensive car I had ever owned was now a battered, mud-splattered wreck. Every panel was dented, the wing mirrors were hanging loose, and grass and mud covered it from the tyres to the roof.

My Datsun Laurel was a mess. This started a journey that would teach me a lesson God had for me; it would reach far beyond car ownership and into every part of my life and ministry.

Ann had been taking the kids to a school concert but had lost control of the car and rolled it into a farmer's field. It was a top-of-the-range automatic with a large engine. Amazingly, no one was hurt but the car ended up back on its wheels, and with the help of the local farmer, Ann had it towed to the school where the inspector had called me.

'Don't be mad?' Well, maybe I was a bit. But they were all OK, that's what mattered. And cars are fixable, aren't they? Unfortunately, not this one.

So, a few weeks later, we made our way, with heads low, to a garage to buy the cheapest new car available. By the time the insurance had paid out and I paid off what I owed on the car's HP agreement, there was nothing left.

'Can I get one of these?' I said, indicating the cheapest car on the lot. The salesman's face lit up like Christmas had come early.

'Er, yes,' he said before telling me about the car.

'OK, where do I sign?' I asked and after a few minutes, I was filling in another HP agreement.

'Er, do you want a test drive, sir?' he asked.

I hadn't thought about that, so I agreed. He handed me a set of keys for his own car, which was the same model, and parked outside.

'Give her a good run, and I will have all the paperwork sorted by the time you get back.'

I had never driven one before. Cheap wasn't the right word. The carpets were thin and rough, there was hardly any sophistication in the cab, and the whole thing felt so different from my beautiful Datsun Laurel. Notwithstanding the awkwardness, we went on a nice drive around York.

After about twenty minutes, I thought it was about time to go back but I noticed the engine wasn't running smoothly. It coughed and spluttered. I looked in the wing mirror and to my horror, we were leaving a narrow trail of burning petrol on the road behind us. No way! What a disaster. So, after a quick emergency stop, we both piled out onto the pavement just in time to see the salesman's car burst into flames at the side of the road. By the time the fire brigade came, the tyres were all aflame and billowing black smoke.

One frantic phone call later and the salesman arrived to collect us. I'm not sure who was more embarrassed. However, I felt I had no other choice but to return to the garage and sign the papers for my new car. Because of the nightmare test drive, he threw in a free sunroof and a tow bar for us. The next day we realised we had made the national papers. We read a fabulous headline we will never forget: 'Test Drive a New Hot Rod, Sir?'

I know it seems mad to sign the papers, but we honestly didn't have a choice. This was the only way I was going to get a car. In the end, though, we loved it and it took us across Europe on holidays. It owed us nothing and a few years later, we gave it away to a friend who had just passed her test; she ran it for years.

My kids were mortified when we took that cheap car home, and it got worse when we needed a second car for Ann and we bought a lime green, ancient Lada. The kids refused to be collected from school in either car.

When I could afford it, I eventually traded the Lada for a Toyota Celica sports car. It had pop-up head lights. Again, I just loved this car but I was starting to realise something. We don't own anything; these are all gifts from God we are simply allowed to use.

A year later, Mark Simons, the Anglican vicar who was my friend and mentor, was going on a three-month sabbatical to Scotland. I felt God give me a gentle prompt to help him as he had helped me so much in dealing with life. He and his wife only had one car so I decided to offer him one of ours for the duration of his trip. Puffing out my chest, I said he could have the sports car. He was amazed by my generosity and I had a nice warm glow about me. Until I put the car keys into his hand and God clearly spoke to me saying, 'That's the last time you will see that car.'

Three weeks later, the vicar rang me to say he had written the car off. A doctor who was travelling in the opposite direction had fallen asleep at the wheel and ploughed straight into him. They were both fine, but the car was not.

So, what was the lesson? Hold everything lightly. We are only guardians of what we have, and things can go at a moment's notice. That applies both to people and to stuff. Later, in ministry, we discovered that the people we spent the most time with were often the ones likely to walk away and hurt you. We are just shepherds, but they are his sheep. It's our job to love and care for them while not clinging on too tightly.

And that included my career. Back in 1993, I was at the start of my breaking.

Chapter Twelve

Face to Face with a Murderer

In 1993, a key highlight for detectives was the twelve-week CID (Criminal Investigation Department) course in Birmingham. Some had been collecting a 'secret fund', which wives and girlfriends didn't know about, to be used for the excessive drinking bouts. Others, including myself, saw it as an opportunity to sharpen their skills and learn as much as they could. The CID course was a residential course, hosted near Edgbaston Cricket Club. The first night, we went to a local pub which had cameras on the outside so the staff could see if there was a police raid. It was a local copper's favourite and it was an eyeopener to see how some of them behaved in their own time. Policing was a very different animal in the mid-nineties.

For the weeks in Birmingham, we would drive down on a Sunday night and go home after Friday afternoon lectures. It was the longest Ann and I had been separated during our marriage, and I seem to remember her taking the chance to get some decorating done in our through-lounge. The paint tin said terracotta, but it lied. When I arrived home, I was faced with a glowing bright orange, a colour we were stuck with for years.

When I was about halfway through the course, I was asleep at home one Saturday night when it just so happened that the phone rang at 1 a.m. The control room officer reported a murder and I was required at Bridlington Police Station. I made my way to Bridlington, where I was told that the body of a man was found in the middle of the road in Flamborough.

The detective sergeant walked into the office and said, 'What are you doing here? You're on your CID course. You shouldn't have been called into work.'

Yet there I was.

It turned out that a taxi driver from Bridlington had been on his way back after dropping a fare in Flamborough and found the body in the road by the church. Sarge suggested that before I went home, I may as well make myself useful and take the taxi driver's statement. I wouldn't be involved in the investigation because I would be back on the CID course the following day.

It took me forty minutes to take down the statement. It just so happened that while I was in the interview room, there was a knock at the door. A uniformed officer said that someone had arrived at the police station who wanted to talk about the death. That was when I came face to face with the murderer.

He was a young, nineteen-year-old man from Flamborough. He said he had been to Bridlington Hospital to deal with a cut on his hand and he wanted to chat with someone about the death in Flamborough. I radioed the detective sergeant and was told, 'This looks like a traffic accident, so we won't be dealing with it. Traffic officers will take over the investigation. Unless this man is driving a car, just take his details and let him go.'

The police are taught to keep their eyes open for the abnormal or the absence of the 'normal'. As a Christian,

I believe that God is interested in every part of my life. The Bible suggests that God empowers us in all aspects of our life (Philippians 4:13; Ephesians 6:10). Over the years, I believe God has given me an ability to accurately identify when things are not right. This was one of those occasions.

So, instead of letting him go, I sat this young man down and took a detailed witness statement from him. His story was bizarre to say the least. He said he worked in a local pub in Flamborough and had been there all night. It had been a quiet night, with just the local regulars in, and he had left at closing time. He went home on his bike, where he decided to make a sandwich, but while he was cutting a tomato, he sliced his hand with the knife. He showed me a small plaster on his left hand. As he explained he took a taxi the six miles to Bridlington Hospital, I thought to myself, 'Did that really need an expensive taxi ride?'

While he was telling his story, I sent a uniformed officer to the hospital to check if his story was true. It turned out he had been to the hospital, although there was a discrepancy with the timing; he arrived at the hospital later than he told me. The hospital also said the cut was superficial.

He said that during another taxi ride back home, the driver told him about the discovery of the body, which was now, according to local gossip, thought to have been caused by a hit-and-run driver. When he arrived home again, he sat for a while and began to worry. He said he had sat wondering if he had served the hit-and-run driver too much alcohol at the pub. However, when I asked for details, he said it had been a quiet night and he couldn't remember anyone. He told me that his brother was killed by a hit-and-run driver years ago and so it was weighing on his mind.

After thinking about this issue for some time he said he decided he needed to cycle to Bridlington to talk to me.

He said he tried to ride by the scene of the accident in Flamborough but was stopped by a special constable. Again, I contacted the detective sergeant, who repeated that it was only a traffic accident and I should finish off and go home. Although I wasn't entirely satisfied with his reasoning for coming to the station, I completed the witness statement. I then decided to fill in a Personal Descriptive Form, itemising all his clothes and the make and colour of his jacket, trainers and bike. His whole account didn't feel right. He went on his way, I came home, returned to the CID course and didn't think anything more about it. After all, it was only a traffic accident.

When the CID course was completed, I returned to Bridlington and was back into the swing of things. The CID investigate the most serious offences. Generally, crimes are reported to the uniform branch, who take the initial calls. Often, for example, with a burglary, uniformed officers visit the house and fill in a crime report with details about how the offence happened.

These daily crime reports would then be allocated. Sometimes they were investigated by the initial officer, but crimes of a more serious nature would go up to the CID Office, where a detective sergeant (DS) would allocate them to one of his detective constables (DCs). The most serious crimes would be investigated by the DSs themselves. In the CID in Bridlington at the time, there were two DSs and four DCs. We would then investigate the crimes over several days or weeks, until all avenues had been exhausted. At which point the crime would have been solved or shelved as unresolved. My clear-up rate was about 30 per cent.

On my return from my CID course, I was presented with a few crimes to investigate. Should I need help, I would ask one of the other DCs to give me a hand to perhaps help with interviews or arrest a suspect. Generally, each DC handled their own crimes so although we knew what others were doing, we didn't always know all the crimes they were investigating.

During those first couple of weeks, nothing much changed. A female DC in another unit was investigating a nasty rape with not much to go on; a young girl had been attacked under the stands of the local football club in Bridlington and there were no witnesses. There had also been a couple of arson attacks on cars in the same area. One of our other DCs was complaining that he had a problem. The DS had told him to get rid of some clothing from a crime by returning it to the victim's family. Our property office was full of items, many that were still needed, but some could be returned. The family refused to take the clothing from him and were starting to question how the case was proceeding. It just so happened it was the family of the Flamborough victim, whose body had been found dead in the middle of the road.

Because of my involvement earlier, I began asking questions about the progress of the investigation myself. I was surprised to find out the cause of death was recorded as an accident, not a traffic accident. It was deemed an accidental death because he died by inhaling his own vomit and choking on it. The family simply couldn't understand how such a regular heavy drinker, walking back from his own birthday party, would vomit and then die from inhaling it at the side of the road. To make matters worse, they were also questioning why his wallet had been found almost a mile away in the central village phone box.

After quite a lengthy meeting, we decided we would take another look at the file. I remember that morning so well. I was sitting with other officers, eating bacon sandwiches, as I looked at the file for the first time. We were a team of experienced detectives who could see straight away that something was wrong. This had started as a sudden death and was designated a traffic accident, yet now, it was being called natural courses, but the file shouted, 'Murder!'

We sat looking at the crime scene photos and could clearly see a few marks across the face of the dead man, in the form of wavy lines. The notes in the file suggested these were made by the herringbone pattern on his own jacket, but to us, these just didn't seem to match.

His wallet was handed in by a local woman from Flamborough who claimed she found it in the phone box the day after the death. When we checked her statement, we realised she had given the same address as that young man I interviewed. Later enquiries discovered she had used her maiden name; she was, in fact, his mother.

By now, we realised this had suddenly become a big case and one of the DSs took on the investigation. The forensic laboratories were contacted, who enlarged and enhanced the crime scene photos over the next few weeks. When the huge six-by-four-foot photos arrived at the office, it was obvious the marks across the face were a footprint. He had been stamped on. With this information, the pathologist revised his earlier findings explaining how that blow to the face could have been enough for the man to vomit and choke. These facts led us straight back to my cyclist.

Two days after the body had been found, that young man had reported his bike stolen. It had later been handed in at Bridlington Police Station and was simply sitting in our bike store waiting to be claimed. Because I had noted the details of his bike on the Personal Descriptive Form (PDF), we knew it was his. There was also blood and DNA evidence under the brake leavers from the cut on his hand.

It turned out he never had a brother. Eventually his mother admitted she had found the wallet in their house, not in the phone box. A search of the house found the jacket I had described in the PDF in huge detail, including the piping down the sleeve. The search also found his trainers which were sent to the forensic lab where the pattern on the sole was matched to the imprint on the dead man's face. Two fibres from the jacket were found on the victim's herringbone jacket, still in its sealed evidence bag. It was just as well my colleague had not returned the jacket to the family. If it had been, the chain of evidence would have broken, and the case would not have gone to court.

As the cyclist had lied to me about the time he was at the hospital, we were able to go ahead with the case. We were able to prove that the victim never went to the pub where the young man worked that night; it was a quiet night, so there was no chance fibres from his jacket could have accidentally transferred onto the victim's clothing.

At last, he was arrested and interviewed by a DI and a DS. Due to my early involvement in the case, I was kept out of the later investigation so as not to contaminate evidence. Throughout the interviews, the man only said, 'No comment.' To try and get him to talk, I was brought into the interview room to read his original statement and the Personal Descriptive Form. Still, he continued to reply, 'No comment.' He was then charged with murder. At Hull Crown Court, he pleaded 'not guilty', but said little in his own defence and never gave any account of his actions. On the strength of the evidence, he was found guilty and sentenced to life imprisonment. I was commended by the judge who said, 'If it hadn't been for bright Bobby Wilks, this case would never have been solved.'

I was just glad I had been instrumental in ensuring the family of the victim got the justice they deserved and that the murderer was convicted and sentenced. God calls us to stand up for the oppressed, to seek justice and to uphold what is right. I praise the Lord for the many times I have known his help and guidance over the years.

On a side note, five years after the Flamborough murder case, I was notified of a cold case review on the rape of the girl at Bridlington Football Club. The DNA taken at the time from the scene matched that of our murderer; he was charged and convicted of that too.

Chapter Thirteen

Never Off Duty

Being a policeman is a vocation, not a job. We carried our warrant cards everywhere we went. In those days, the warrant cards were simple pieces of typed blue cardboard that fit snuggly into an ordinary wallet but they carried all the authority of the crown behind them. This meant I was never truly off duty. After all my years of being a rural bobby, I learnt that villagers would turn up at the office when it suited them, not when I was on shift. Whenever Ann and I wanted time for ourselves, we made a deliberate point of getting out of the village. This principle of taking time for each other has stood us in good stead in our years of ministry, as once again, we realised that setting time aside for ourselves is what keeps a healthy marriage. We have always let our people know we are available for them, no matter what time of day, if there is an emergency. More than once we've had frantic phone calls in the early hours of the morning, asking for help or a visit.

One Christmas Eve, when we lived in Stamford Bridge, the phone rang at nearly midnight. We didn't have a phone by the bed in those days, so I stumbled out in my pyjamas. I ran downstairs, bumping into the presents we had so carefully arranged in the lounge just a few hours earlier, and picked up the receiver. I heard the apologetic voice of the 999-control-room operator in Hull apologising for disturbing me but there was a policeman in trouble in Stamford Bridge. He had called for help, but unfortunately, the nearest available car was more than half an hour away.

I was glad I hadn't been drinking. I grabbed my car keys and ran out, still in my pyjamas and slippers, and drove to the centre of the village. There, I saw a colleague struggling with a prisoner. They were both laid across the bonnet of his police car with the prisoner on top of him, hitting him repeatedly. But the bobby wouldn't let go. He had been there for some time, trying to subdue him. The prisoner was high on drugs and drug-users seem to have superhuman strength. There was a burglary and a neighbour, who had been out to midnight mass, called the police. Together, we placed the guy in the car and set off on a fifty-minute drive in icy conditions, to Goole Police Station.

My colleague needed to visit the minor injuries unit in the local hospital after we waited for the offender to be processed. As a result, I unfortunately had to wait a considerable time for another car to take me home. The station wasn't exactly warm and I was shivering as I let myself into the house at 4 a.m. I was creeping up the stairs, trying not to wake anyone, when I heard a little voice saying, 'Daddy, has Santa been yet?'

I didn't get much sleep that day.

A few years later, while we were living in Driffield, I was taking my dog on a walk. It was autumn and we had just put the clocks back, so although it was early evening, it was already dark. Ann had taken Philip out for the evening, so Rachel and I put Sheba on the lead and left the house. Rachel would have been eight or nine years old and Sheba was our black Lab Border Collie. It wasn't often Rachel and I got to go anywhere just the two of us, so we were looking forward to it. We took a left at the bottom of the street, but it soon became obvious we weren't going far.

Just around the corner, in a darkened driveway, three men were crouching down by the side of a car. They tried to move further into the darkness, but I recognised them as local youths and called out. I could see they were syphoning petrol from the vehicle. Two of them immediately fled, leaving the third holding the petrol can. I told him he was under arrest and pushed him to the wall to corral him while shouting at Rachel to run home with the dog and call the police. She turned and high-tailed it back.

It was early evening and there was no one else around to call on for help. The youth was becoming more and more irate, struggling to get free. I quickly realised no one was coming to help me. In a final act of defiance, the youth emptied the petrol over my head; the liquid ran down my face and covered my leather jacket. As I knew him, I decided to let him go rather than risking him lighting the fuel and setting me on fire.

I returned home to find Rachel crying by the phone; she didn't know what to do. I consoled her before we walked to the police station and reported the incident. She sat in the foyer while I spoke to the officers. I had to leave my jacket as evidence. Because this was considered a possible arson offence, it had to be encased and sealed within one of the thick, crispy nylon evidence bags. Normally, clothing would be stored in plastic bags, but as plastic is made from petrol, the fumes could contaminate any evidence on my coat. I collected Rachel as the officers left to arrest the young men. I do remember it being extremely cold as we walked home that night. It had not been the evening together we'd hoped for. I had nothing further to do with the incident. I don't even know if the lads were charged, but I got my coat back several months later, still smelling of petrol.

For many years, we had holidays in Devon. We found a lovely farm where we stayed on several occasions. The family were friendly, and the children loved to feed the livestock. We had driven into Barnstaple one morning and parked near the shopping centre when I noticed a local PC struggling to arrest a shoplifter. Television always makes it look so easy, but trying to put handcuffs on a determined offender is harder than it seems. American television programmes often feature the offence of 'resisting arrest' as a crime in itself, which leads to extra punishment. However, here in England, there is no such law so criminals regularly make it difficult for policemen to put both hands into the cuffs.

I rushed over and identified myself as an off-duty officer, producing my warrant card. I helped to subdue the perpetrator and we took him to the local station. Then, of course, I had to hunt down Ann and the kids in the days before mobile phones. We had a favourite spot on the sand at Westward Ho by the rusting shipwreck, and I soon joined them for sandwiches on the beach.

It wasn't always me who got involved in tailing a criminal. One springtime, Ann and I took a trip to Scarborough, outside our force area. We were walking through the main shopping area when I spotted a familiar face. I ducked into a shop doorway, pulling Ann with me.

I called the local police station to report my sighting of a jewel thief who was on warrant for burglary. They said they would send someone as soon as they could, but could I keep an eye on him? That was difficult, because as I recognised him, I was pretty sure he would recognise me too. If he saw me, I knew that he would run, and I didn't want to spend my day off running through Scarborough after him.

I came up with a cunning plan. I slipped off my anorak and gave it to Ann. In one of the pockets was a dark brown beanie hat I had been wearing most of the winter when walking Sheba. I suggested Ann pull it well down on her head. She had a couple of plastic bags in her pocket and I filled them with scrunched up newspaper from a bin. Off she went, my very own 'bag lady'. She was able to keep the thief in sight, sauntering along unobtrusively a few yards behind him. I kept close, only a hundred yards behind, until the local guys came to take over pursuit. We left them to it; the suspect was not someone I wanted to notice my involvement.

Many years later, we had left the police and were working for Pastor Paul Epton when we were travelling from Stamford Bridge to Gate Helmsley. We had a couple of friends in the car with us. It was early evening, we had been to a service together and the roads were wet.

The car in front suddenly swerved and spun into the nearside verge, twisting and turning until it ended up in the gutter, facing us. I immediately jumped from the car, shouting at my friend to ring 999 and ask for the fire brigade and ambulance. I could already see flames from beneath the bonnet. I glanced back and I don't think I'll ever forget the look of horror on my friends' faces as I ran towards the burning vehicle. The driver's door was jammed so I got into the car via the passenger door as flames continued to engulf the engine. I started to cautiously pull the driver out from the burning wreck. He was unconscious and seemed to be badly injured. I carefully got him out of the car as a neighbour from one of the houses opposite came running out with a fire extinguisher.

We managed to put out the fire before it engulfed the driver's compartment. I sat on the grass, holding the driver and supporting him until the ambulance arrived. Just another day at the office, or not. Those days in the police office were behind me, but those instincts to help someone, even if it means running towards danger, will always be ingrained within me.

Chapter Fourteen

Organised Crime

Most of the time, criminals work alone, and their crimes are often 'spur of the moment' offences. However, sometimes there are incidents described as 'organised crime': committed by people who may be called 'speciality criminals' or professional criminals.

For months, we had been aware of such a group operating in and around the East Yorkshire area. They specialised in breaking into premises and removing safes; they were well organised and prepared. Their MO (modus operandi) was to steal a safe from a solicitor's office, post office or even a cash dispenser. They would remove the safe from the scene and then open it at another location. This meant they were in and out of buildings fast – before uniformed officers could respond to any triggered alarms. They also had 'spotters' using two-way radios to report any police movement alongside people cutting telephone wires. So, if an alarm was activated, it couldn't go through to the police or the alarm company. Sometimes, they would use ladders to climb up the side of buildings to drill holes in the outside alarm box and fill it with expanding foam, thus deadening the sound.

The group was very successful. However, they didn't know we had an informant feeding us the details about when and where these jobs were happening. Informants are usually criminals who, for various reasons, report to the police on the criminal activities of others. Sometimes, informants want to get rid of competitors while others look to rise up through their gang ranks, but most of the time, they want the money. Good informants get paid well by the police and by insurance companies when goods are recovered.

So, we knew who the gang members were and we had started making arrests as the offences took place. The leaders often got away by using 'lesser' criminals to do the dirty work.

We knew them, and they knew us. It sometimes felt like a game of cat and mouse. Who would be the first to win? We heard, through the informant, that the gang had put a bounty on finding the home addresses of the Bridlington CID officers. Their aim was to create fear, so we would stop our investigations. They planned to burgle the officers' homes, trash the houses and frighten us and our families. It wouldn't have been uncommon for them to try and follow us home from the office to get our addresses. As a result, we needed to keep our eyes open and often deliberately take different routes home.

I was working in Bridlington but living in another nearby town. I was well-known in the community, both because of my role in the police and as an active Christian, volunteering in local schools and youth clubs. However, over several weeks, God supernaturally protected us. The criminals knew my car and who I was, but somehow, they never found out where I lived.

Some of the gang members were on probation for earlier offences. They needed to attend the local office to meet with their probation officer. It just so happened that the probation office was a mere hundred yards from my home. On a few occasions, I was getting into my car with guitar, keyboard, and a couple of children in tow when these criminals would arrive in their vehicles. They walked almost past my house, but time and time again, they failed to recognise me or my car and so didn't know my address. Eventually, we successfully caught most of the gang and their crime spree came to an end.

When I joined the police, having clearly heard God's voice to do so, I knew the Lord would have other plans for me at some stage. As the years went on, each time I sustained an injury, and there were a few of them, I wondered if it would be the one to see me leave the police. However, it never seemed to happen.

I had been to university and so it was always expected I would be promoted up the ranks. But I felt that God called me to the streets, not to the office. Throughout my career, I stayed as a constable and never went for promotion as I wanted to remain on the frontline. Although I knew my calling was to the streets, I did take every opportunity for additional training. I was always looking for ways to learn. I developed new interviewing skills, attended exhibits officer training, and ultimately trained to become a detective in the CID. That took me to the CID in Bridlington, from where I was often sent out to major investigations throughout the county.

One of the specialist courses I completed was the H.O.L.M.E.S. system – the Home Office Large Major Enquiry System.

H.O.L.M.E.S. was an innovative computer system for indexing major incidents. In the past, most major incidents had been indexed on physical cards which had to be manhandled, read and compared to find links between their various pieces of information. H.O.L.M.E.S. allowed an officer to file an address and link it to a witness statement, a work address, a club or pub the person visits, the clothes they were wearing and the car they drive, including the colour, make and model. Later, if officers want to know something about what happened on the same street as a pub, they can instantly see who could have been there.

This new system of indexing was for major incidents only and was used by each police force independently. When a murder or other major crime happened, a member of the H.O.L.M.E.S. team would set up an incident room for the duration of the enquiry, until the perpetrator was found. The H.O.L.M.E.S. programme would generate 'actions' and these would be sent to detectives who would complete the specific jobs. One example was to Trace, Identify and Eliminate (TIE) the man in the red jumper who appeared in one of the witness statements. After the detectives had been out, they'd return with some information that needed indexing, until finally, all the details would lead to an arrest and conviction.

The CID are responsible for investigating the most serious crimes. I was no longer sent out to arrest shoplifters but instead, we were tasked to investigate burglaries and even more major incidents. We were each allocated crimes to investigate, quite often working independently, but sometimes we had a partner. In the case of a murder, a whole murder squad would form to investigate the crime. Those murder enquiries could take months before we were released back to our own station. We went wherever we were needed; I have been part of teams in Howden, Hull, Bridlington, as well as the prison riots at Full Sutton.

We were always encouraged to find our *own* sources of intelligence, and to cultivate informants who were paid to tell us about both planned and committed crimes in the local area. Each CID officer would develop as many informants as possible. To protect their identity, the informant's name would be known only to the officer and one other person. Other intelligence could arrive by many other sources, and if it wasn't urgent, it would land in a tray in the DS's office and wait for a rainy day.

Chapter Fifteen

Storms of Life

One wet Thursday, I had returned from a murder enquiry and hadn't been allocated to any crimes. I had finished off the last of my paperwork and glanced out of the window. Dark clouds had been brooding over the skyline for most of the morning and large droplets of rain were beginning to chase each other down the glass. With no other work to do, it just so happened that I decided to look in the 'Rainy Day Tray' to see if anything caught my attention. The thunder crashed and the lightning forked across the sky as I walked into the detective sergeant's office. Little did I know what lay ahead and what storms I'd have to walk through in the months ahead.

I remember sitting in the office alone and opening an envelope. Inside was a letter, another envelope, and a routing slip to show where the letter had been. It was a handwritten letter. One page long. It had been addressed to someone in the USA, the return address was a post office box in London, but the telephone number had a Humberside prefix. The letter was thanking the recipient for his enquiries about the photos and that the albums were available, including the ones of 'the younger kind'. It then suggested the recipient could get in touch to discuss the matter further. The letter had been intercepted by the USA postal service, forwarded to Interpol, who then sent it to Scotland Yard. And because of the Humberside phone number, the letter eventually arrived at our office.

The tone of the letter made it clear that someone was distributing indecent images of children. It was 1996. The internet was in its infancy and computers were still mostly in offices and not for personal use. No detective that I spoke to had ever dealt with anything like this. We did have a child abuse unit, but that dealt with children who were victims of physical abuse. This was entirely different.

A three-year enquiry began. It would take me the length and breadth of the country and I would liaise with police forces across counties. I started by working with the paedophile unit at Scotland Yard, who had some experience with this type of offence. They told me the PO box was in regular use as a drop box and large quantities of letters were held there until they were collected. The telephone number from the letter was traced as a second line to a large, detached house on the outskirts of town. After a couple of months, we obtained a search warrant and the house was raided. I led the team of both uniformed officers and detectives. The house was home to a middle-aged professional man and his sixteen-year-old Filipino house-boy.

When the boy was interviewed, we discovered he had come to England two years before as an illegal immigrant and was being used as a live-in servant. Because of his illegal status, immigration officers took him away before we had chance to interview him properly. Unfortunately, we couldn't ask him for the exact details of what had been happening in the house, but we were pretty sure he was also there as a sex-slave.

In an upstairs bedroom, which had been turned into an office, we found lots of filing cabinets. These contained hundreds of photos featuring naked men. There were often multiple copies of each photo and many had been compiled into groups. There were also boxes of VHS video tapes. One filing cabinet was full of letters the owner had received and he had itemised which photos he had sold to each buyer. Among the photos were several of naked boys and many letters were requesting more of these younger photographs. Hundreds of people were asking for material; it was the days before any homosexual pornography was readily available. We seized everything, arrested the man and quickly interviewed him but he was released on bail, due to return to the police station in four weeks' time.

I began itemising every single photo and letter, giving each one a unique reference number. As I said, there were hundreds of photos and a whole filing cabinet of itemised letters from his customers. It quickly became apparent this would become a huge investigation.

Over the coming months, I produced a comprehensive list of the clients specifically asking for images of young boys. Sometimes, these requests were for photos of very young boys. It was beyond anything I had ever dealt with. At that time, no one else in Humberside had dealt with anything similar. I soon found myself liaising with the New Scotland Yard paedophile unit, the National Crime Intelligence Service, and attending training courses with other forces who dealt with the secret world of child pornography.

A few months later, police officers from multiple forces simultaneously executed search warrants at the homes of the people on my list. Further evidence from these searches led to the uncovering of a nationwide paedophile network. Its demographic was not the typical, spotty-faced criminals people might have expected; many of them were middle-aged, wealthy gentlemen with powerful connections.

Many had taken great care to hide their material. For example, a three-hour video labelled as a collection of mundane television programmes could include a short video of children being abused in the middle of the tape. Lists of contacts were hidden under floorboards and even behind electric sockets, making the house searches difficult. We often needed specialist search teams to retrieve the articles.

For several weeks, I travelled across the country to other police forces to review any seized material and identify whether it had come from our man in Humberside. The same material was found in multiple homes, suggesting a nationwide network of distributors existed. I don't need to give any details, but some of the material was horrendous and caused great distress to view and catalogue.

Over subsequent years, I became an expert in this type of offence and was involved in at least two other similar investigations. There's a certain level of excitement that comes with an involvement in these larger cases but the toll it takes on an officer's mental health can be disastrous.

Chapter Sixteen

Lost in Fear

It was no surprise that the continuous exposure to disturbing and graphic images affected my own mental health. The practice of dealing with this kind of crime was new, and support or counselling simply didn't exist in those days. I was expected to 'suck it up' and carry on.

One sunny afternoon during this investigation, I was called into the office for a meeting with a DS. One look at his drawn face told me he was about to give me a crime of terrible nature. The body of a baby, only a few weeks old, had been found in a shoebox on someone's doorstep. We arrived at the scene to recover the body and it was taken for examination in a specialist unit at the hospital while we started door-to-door enquiries. A short while later, a woman in a nearby house admitted the baby was hers. We took her to a specialist social services unit for interview; I sat outside for about an hour as the social worker and my sergeant talked to her.

Because I was a trained exhibits officer, I was tasked with thoroughly searching her house. It turned out she gave birth to the baby alone several months before. She already had a six-year-old son but had kept this pregnancy and birth a secret. The baby was kept in the shoebox, locked in a cupboard, and she would occasionally feed and change it. She would take her son on long weekends with other members of her family and leave the baby alone in the house, until sadly, it died.

Another DC and I spent two long days searching the house for evidence to confirm her story. We recovered other shoeboxes, items of baby clothing, and even the stretch of bloodstained carpet where she'd given birth. The house was full of food with many items being out of date. It seemed this woman had suffered from some sort of mental breakdown, resulting in her baby starving to death. What we had to deal with profoundly affected both me and the other constable. In fact, he went off sick a few weeks later. After we finished searching the house, we simply went home. There was no counselling. No one to talk to. The image of 'macho policemen' was maintained and we were expected to get on with it.

Early the following morning, I received a phone call from the office about another major incident. An elderly lady was sexually attacked on a piece of open ground near to her home in Bridlington. She had been taken to hospital but was not expected to survive. She died shortly afterwards, and this became a murder enquiry. I was allocated the job of talking to her next-door neighbour, who initially was the prime suspect. Although he remained a person of interest, the case was never resolved. However, the interviews uncovered a plethora of drug use, alcohol abuse and child abuse in the neighbourhood. Here came another 'can of worms.'

It was during this enquiry I started to see things slipping with my own mental health. I was still completing the various paedophile cases by preparing the materials and paperwork so it was ready for the upcoming court cases. It all came to a head one Sunday. Our church rented a community hall and every week before the service, all the sound equipment had to be set up and the chairs laid out. This week, I was on the rota to help with the PA set up.

As I started to unpack the van, it was as though a sudden thunderstorm crashed around in my head. Images from the paedophile enquiry were so vivid in the forefront of my mind – material I hadn't thought about for months. A real sense of rage descended. I was angry with the perpetrators and at my own helplessness towards the children looking out from those photographs.

I knew I needed to leave. Soon I would start throwing things around. It was as if some floodgates had opened. The moment I stopped, I was totally overwhelmed with all I had seen and done in the last three years. These were the first outward manifestations of PTSD (Post Traumatic Stress Disorder).

To be that angry all the time was frightening. I vividly remember those sweat-drenched nights, being angry, traumatised and one step away from being sent to a specialist hospital. I constantly suffered with the thought of 'here we go again'. The rage would slowly build, starting at my feet, before crawling its way up my body.

The slow, rhythmical, peaceful sound of Ann sleeping beside me did nothing to quell the fear that accompanied the rage. Rage, for what I had become. Anger, almost uncontrollable, eating away at my insides. I'd have a sheen of sweat on my body as the images flashed across my mind like a never-ending news reel. Every time I closed my eyes, it was pressing play on the worst videos I'd ever had to watch. I would experience the helplessness I felt because I couldn't do anything to change the torment on their faces as they were being abused. It was all so overwhelming.

The rage would grow and become a living, breathing thing. Could I let go and allow it to take full control? If I did, could I do it? Could I get the furniture through the bedroom window and throw it haphazardly into the streets below? Would succumbing to the rage be the release I needed? Or should I simply walk away and leave Ann and the kids? Surely it wasn't fair on them? All the mood swings and violent outbursts became our life during that time. I had a need to never be out of Ann's sight. The panic attacks were debilitating enough, but the inability to sleep without her holding me like a child was hard. I felt as if I shouldn't have needed this as a strong man. Worse still were the hours of silence, sitting staring into space. The one-hundred-yard stare that words could not penetrate.

Eventually, the breakdown came. There I was sitting at home, to all intents and purposes a broken man, unable to function in any of the roles that mattered to me: husband, father, church member, policeman, friend. We used to sing a little chorus by Daniel Iverson:

> Spirit of the living God, fall afresh on me.
> Break me, melt me, mould me, fill me . . .[2]

This was what it was like to be broken. PTSD manifests differently in different people. If I lost sight of Ann for a few seconds, I would have a panic attack. She became my rock. If she walked around the corner of a display in a shop, I would run outside frantically, unable to breathe. For eighteen months, this became our way of life. I was unable to drive for more than half an hour without the need to crawl into the back of the car and sleep. I literally couldn't read anything displayed vertically, like a menu outside a restaurant or a

---

2. Copyright © 2004 Birdwing Music/EMI CMP/Small Stone Media/Song Solutions Daybreak info@songsolutions.org & Thankyou Music/Adm. By worshiptogether.com songs excl. UK & Europe adm at IntegrityRights.com

notice in the street. I could no longer count beyond twelve or so; I would lose track of where I was and had to start again. This meant I could no longer do the household finances, a job I had always taken pride in. I was subject to uncontrollable anger and would often weep. I could not look at a baby for months and whenever I heard a parent raise their voice at their children, I would find tears streaming down my face.

My sleep patterns were disturbed. Most afternoons I would lie on the sofa, my head on Ann's lap as she read to me, until I eventually fell asleep. She read all three volumes of *The Lord of the Rings* in this way. At night whenever I did manage to fall asleep in Ann's arms, she would move gently over in the bed and pray through words from Scriptures, hymns or songs she had memorised, but wouldn't risk waking me by turning the light on.

The police sent me to various trauma specialists, psychologists and psychiatrists. Although they were able to deal with the nightmares, nothing else really improved. I was a mess. I could hardly sleep and most days I would just sit vacantly staring at the walls. Yet somehow, I knew through it all, God was with me. When I joined the police because of God's call, I believed it was for a season. He would eventually call me out into something different. Was this it?

At first, church people would visit and pray for me but as the weeks slipped into months, they slowly stopped coming. If they saw us in the street, sometimes they would cross the road to avoid us, keeping their eyes downcast, making me feel as if they were embarrassed to talk to us.

During that time, as the police were deciding what to do with me, I tried a phased return to work where I went into the CID office for an hour a day. However, once again, all I seemed able to do was stare at the walls or out the window. When my GP heard about it, he immediately signed me off sick again.

So, eventually, the decision was made that I would leave the police. In my heart of hearts, I knew it was right. I knew that I simply couldn't carry on. That big, strong, capable and fearless man wasn't there anymore. So, we waited for the long process of dismissal to take its bureaucratic time.

The weeks went by slowly, until a friend just so happened to tell me he was going to Sheffield for a Reinhard Bonnke meeting in a football stadium. Reinhard was a South African evangelist with a well-known healing ministry. My friend, Kim, the best man at our wedding, had lived in South Africa and worked as an electrician on some of the huge crusades Reinhard held, so they knew each other personally. He arranged to take me with him and to introduce us at the end of the meeting so Reinhard could pray for me. My friend had promised not to leave my side as I had not been out of Ann's sight for almost two years.

Could this be the answer? Would this result in my healing and allow me to return to the police?

So, off we went, with great expectation for this to be the turning point in my recovery. I expected healing and to be back to the man I once was within days. I expected angels and a powerful encounter with God – only that would fix me. The Lord must have been smiling because his plans were so different from mine. Isaiah 55:8-9 says: '"For my thoughts are not your thoughts, neither are your ways my ways," declares the LORD. "As the heavens are higher than the earth, so are my ways higher than your ways and my thoughts than your thoughts."'

We sat at the back of the football stadium on the raised bleachers as the meeting started. A stage had been built on the pitch and the stadium was almost full, a worship band played some great upbeat music, and then Reinhard came on to speak. The air was buzzing with anticipation as he talked about healings he'd seen and the thousands who had come to faith. It was a simple message and he called people forward to accept Christ as their Saviour before calling people forward for prayer. I sat expectantly, waiting for him to call me forward, but it never happened. The rest was a blur. The meeting ended and Kim pushed his way through the departing crowds while keeping me close. He talked his way past the security team and eventually found Reinhard about to leave through the rear door to get into a waiting car.

Kim spent a few moments reminiscing with Reinhard and then reminded him about me. He seemed in an incredible rush, so he simply laid his hand on my head and prayed that in Jesus' name I would be healed. Then he walked off, got into his car, and told Kim he'd ring him for a catch-up later. It was certainly not the powerful encounter I had expected.

We returned home and life carried on the same as before. Four weeks passed. Four weeks to the day I was sat where I am sitting now as I write, in our own house in Driffield, and suddenly it happened. I blinked and it was as if a switch had been turned on. I knew that God had done something amazing. It was as though I had been living in a dark room that had suddenly filled with light.

The worst was over. The panic attacks stopped and life started to take on a whole new meaning. Let me say straight away I was not the same as I had been, and all these years later, that is still the case. During the early days of the illness, one of the counsellors used an illustration as she was talking to Ann. She said that when all the air is let out of a blown-up balloon, it doesn't look exactly like the balloon it was before. It's the same for people going through PTSD; they will never be the same as they were before.

I liken it to someone who has had an accident and lost an arm; there are just some things they can't do anymore. I had a choice. I could sit around all day and bemoan the fact I was unable to do what I once could, or I could get on and live the best life I could, learning to cope with my disabilities. Years later, there are still things that are tough, but I have learnt to live with them. The superb, confident, hard policeman has gone and a much more compassionate, caring, God-centred man has taken his place. In fact, Ann would say she has a new husband and the children, a new father.

God uses broken people. Even when we are broken and hurting, and even feel rejected as though God has abandoned us, we need to hang in there. The experiences we are going through can make us the ideal person to reach out to others in a similar situation.

Just because we are following what God has told us to do doesn't mean things will be easy. As we're writing this book, we've been thinking about the prophet Elijah in the Old Testament, who prophesied that there would be a drought for years. He had to live through the discomfort of famine himself. First, God sent him to the brook where ravens fed him and he had water to drink, but then the brook dried up. Often, when one door closes, God opens another. Elijah was sent to a poor widow and her son who was expected to die. His obedience to God's prompting and her obedience to Elijah, as the man of God, led to miraculous provision for them both (1 Kings 17). I look back at this time of heartache and famine in my life and can see the hand of God still guiding and directing me.

That was basically the end of my time in the police. Initially, I was off sick, and then they tried to reintegrate me into work by doing short shifts, but after eighteen months they recognised I couldn't carry on. I was diagnosed with PTSD, considered 66 per cent disabled, and invalided out of the force with the maximum invalidity benefit. I was only forty-three years old and my career was in tatters. Yet, through it all, I knew God's hand was still on me and he was still working out his purpose in our lives.

One day, the disciples were sailing across the Sea of Galilee. They were fishermen so this was a familiar experience. However, Galilee is famous for the sudden squalls that descend unexpectedly over the water. This time, it was so fierce that they were in danger of drowning. Jesus was fast asleep at the back of the boat as the wind was howling and the rain lashed down.

The terrified disciples woke him, saying, 'Master, don't you care if we are sinking?'

Jesus simply stood up and commanded the winds and the waves to become calm.

'Peace, be still!' he said. Amazingly, there was immediate peace, but the disciples grew terrified for a different reason. They asked one another, 'Who is this, that even the winds and the waves obey him?' (Mark 4:35-41).

Throughout the disruptions my PTSD caused in our family life, we were sure that the one who controls even the wind and the storm was with us. He would lead us into a new season.

When Ann meditated on words of songs at night during that hard period, she would see God's hand in our journeys and pray that we would really trust him for the future. This was one of the school hymns she used, which talks about life being a journey:

Father, hear the prayer we offer:
not for ease our prayer shall be,
but for strength that we may ever
live our lives courageously.

Not forever in green pastures
would we ask our way to be,
but the steep and rugged pathway
may we tread rejoicingly.

Not forever by still waters
would we idly rest and stay,
but would smite the living fountains
from the rocks along the way.

This hymn was written in the nineteenth century by Love Maria Whitcomb Willis (1824–1908), but the words are just as meaningful today.

PART FOUR

Policeman to Pastor

Chapter Seventeen

A New Direction

The bureaucracy of the police was still dragging on, and a few weeks later, it just so happened that the denomination we belonged to, Elim Pentecostal Churches, was setting up a new evangelistic department led by Rev. Paul Epton from Birkenhead. We wrote to him, congratulating him and saying how pleased we were. After sharing some of our story, he invited us for a visit. We obviously said something in our letter that triggered a God-response within him because it was a surprise he even wrote back. It's often said the doors of history move on the smallest of hinges and that was certainly the case here.

Pastor Paul ran a large city-centre church in Birkenhead. They had purchased what was once a children's hospital and had converted it to meet many different requirements. It had a day nursery, a residential home for the elderly, offices and a large auditorium for the church to meet on a Sunday. The congregation was between three and four hundred people and they worshipped there on a regular basis. It was in his office where we started talking about our future.

We explained about where we were in life at the time. I told him all about why I was leaving the police and Paul sat and listened, nodding encouragement, and occasionally asking the odd clarifying question. At the end of the conversation he said, 'Look, why don't you come and join us here? You can leave whenever you like and if it gets too much, just simply give me a ring and walk away. It'll be fine. You won't be under any stress at all, but I really think you have a lot to offer.'

It was so encouraging that he fully accepted our limitations, assuring us we were free to leave should things become overwhelming.

I have mentioned how much of a strain my illness had put on the family. When we got home and told our sixteen-year-old daughter Rachel, tears sprang into her eyes as she hugged me and said, 'I knew that someone would still need my daddy.' She had apparently heard me during those difficult times when I had expressed a sense of frustration, to the point of having no purpose in my situation.

A few weeks later, we were driving over the Pennines as the early morning mist shrouded a hazy sun. It promised to be a lovely warm day. We were heading back to Birkenhead, this time with our son, Phil. He had just finished A-levels and was looking for something to do for the summer. When Pastor Paul asked for a team to go to Zimbabwe for a couple of weeks' mission with him, Phil responded. He financed the trip by doing a sponsored fast. One thing to know about Phil is that he loves his food. So most of his school mates supported the fast on the assumption he wouldn't be able to do it. However, they were proved wrong and he had an amazing, life-changing experience in Zimbabwe, which caused him to rethink his future. He ended up joining three other young people on a gap year with the EET (the Elim Evangelistic Team).

Ann and I have always been involved in training young people: Ann trained as a teacher at Leeds University, we were both part of the church's youth team as teenagers; we ran kids' clubs, holiday Bible clubs and a successful schools' team who took RE lessons and assemblies in numerous primary schools. We trained a team of teenagers who worked alongside us, taking them on mission to Wales and Cornwall for several years as part of Scripture Union's summer outreach programme. While I was in the police, I trained as a tutor constable, training young detectives to watch and learn before releasing them into the role of detective under my supervision until they were ready to go it alone.

When Phil joined the EET for the gap year programme, we were tasked with supervising this group of four young people. We would train them on how to be self-sufficient as they took on a flat together. We also encouraged them to develop their music and drama gifts for use on the streets and arcades of Wolverhampton. This was part of the evangelistic efforts to establish a church on one of the rougher estates in the city. It was during this time that Phil experienced an incredible answer to prayer over his finances. The other three youngsters were being sponsored by their home churches because they had known they were doing the gap year for months. Phil had only been challenged to join because of the mission to Zimbabwe, so he was very much living by faith. They'd been living in the flat for two or three months when all the utility bills were due at the same time. The other students had their contributions ready, but Phil had no extra cash available. He remembers laying the bills out on the coffee table and kneeling in front of it, spreading his hands over them and simply committing his needs to God. He knew that God had called him to join the team and believed that he was able to supply his needs. We knew nothing about this until the following morning. Phil phoned us to say that a bulging envelope of cash, containing exactly the right amount of money he needed, had been posted through the flat door that morning and was addressed to him. To this day, we don't know who sent it, but it certainly encouraged his faith. He went on to become a youth worker and later took a theology degree before becoming a Baptist pastor in the Midlands. He has grown a small, elderly congregation into a thriving multi-age church. Seven years later, he has more than a hundred people, including many families; he runs a rolling Alpha programme and sees many people come to faith and getting baptised.

While Phil was on the gap year programme, Pastor Paul Epton was contacted by churches all over England to come and help them to grow and reach into their local communities. This meant the EET needed to buy lots of new equipment. Ann and I were in the process of sourcing three fabulous blue and white marquees. Two of them had the capacity to seat 300 people and the third one was huge; it would seat 1200 people at a time. That was only the beginning. Once we had the tents, they needed to be equipped. The list was endless: huge three- and four-foot tent pegs, sledgehammers, guy ropes, and a van to transport everything.

When Paul was back in Birkenhead, we set up one of the tents on the green outside the church and learnt how to erect it. What an adventure that was – learning how to lay out three giant pieces of canvas, one central one and two semicircular ones for the ends. The canvases joined together by short rope loops, and Ann's job would be to slip off her shoes and slot each loop into the next all the way across the join.

Once the tent was up, and it took a team of about a dozen of us to do that, we walked inside this amazing empty space. We realised that though it looked great, we needed even more stuff to fill it. We needed the generator to run the electrics, the lighting and the PA system. We needed a stage and, of course, seats for all the people we hoped would come. But what a great start to our time with the EET.

One of the many things we learnt from Pastor Paul was his incredible work-ethic. When we were preparing for the bigger tent meetings (the crusades), even though he was the speaker on the evenings, we would still see him in his three-piece suit with his jacket off, tie askew and shirtsleeves rolled up, heaving on one of the guy ropes to pull the blue and white canvas up the huge metal poles. Those poles took four people on each, turning the winches and walking the poles inwards as they carried the considerable weight of the fabric. This did tend to attract an audience as we worked.

That wasn't the only way Paul demonstrated his servant's heart. Every Sunday, more than an hour before the church service, he would stand outside the building on the roadside with a plastic bag. Woodchurch Road in Birkenhead was a rough area and with fast-food outlets just down the street, there was always the inevitable litter left by revellers on the Saturday night. Paul would pick it up by hand so the congregation didn't have to walk through it to get into church. The area was so rough that one Saturday night a man was kicked to death on the church doorstep.

Being servant-hearted is certainly an important aspect of Christian leadership, but it does not come easily to some people. We can become too concerned about our rights and privileges, forgetting that we follow the one who 'did not come to be served, but to serve' (Matthew 20:28), and who demonstrated that fact by washing the disciples' feet at the last supper (John 13). I remember we had one young American who wanted to join the EET. He arrived at the beginning of spring as we were preparing all the equipment for that year's tent crusades. He was a worship leader in his church back home and brought his guitar with him. The day after he joined us, we set about filling the trailer with 300 stacking chairs. We'd wheel them out of the storeroom, place them on the tail-lift and then secure them inside the vehicle. Ann, another young man, and I were steadily working our way through the 300, when we suddenly realised the American was not with us. I soon found him, sitting in the back-office fiddling with his guitar. I was not pleased, but I politely asked him to come and give us a hand.

Next came his proud reply, 'But, you see, I'm a worship leader, I don't get involved with that kind of thing.'

I explained that when we are working with the EET, we get involved with whatever needs doing, all of us pull our weight, whatever our other giftings may be. His face fell. That obviously wasn't what he had expected. In fact, he decided that same day that God had called him to leave the EET for somewhere where his giftings would be appreciated.

He left and we never expected to hear from him again. We were so surprised when about twenty years later, we received a letter postmarked from Romania. By that time, this young man was in full-time Christian ministry in Romania and he was writing to us to apologise for his attitude and behaviour all those years ago. He said that our words and example had challenged him for years afterwards, and he now wanted to acknowledge that his short time with us had led to a significant change in his heart. In our minds, we had probably written him off, but isn't it wonderful that God is the God of second chances?

It reminds me of when the Apostle Paul was on his first missionary journey with Barnabas and they had a problem with a young man called John Mark. During their trip, they were all severely mistreated and so the young man left them and returned home. Later, Paul and Barnabas planned to go back and visit the new little churches again. Barnabas wanted to take John Mark, who was his cousin, but Paul was adamant that he would not take him. This led to an argument between Paul and Barnabas which left them estranged for decades. It is wonderful that Scripture records for us that God loves reconciliation and we read that these relationships were eventually restored. Many years later, in his first letter to the Corinthians, Paul writes about both himself and Barnabas in glowing terms as apostles in the early church (1 Corinthians 1:12) and later still, in his last letter (2 Timothy 4:11), he even says how much he relies upon John Mark's help. Thinking about the Apostle Paul reminds me of the amazing things we saw and experienced during our own time on mission, and I will illustrate this through the following stories.

Chapter Eighteen

Does God Heal Today?

Over the next five years, Ann and I relocated to Birkenhead where we lived in a flat within the church complex during the winter months. We worked on collecting the equipment for the tents, as well as helping to produce and distribute evangelistic leaflets and materials that churches could use in their campaigns and missions. As soon as the weather improved, we were out and about with one or more of the marquees helping churches with the Gospel, Miracle and Healing Crusades.

Sometimes, these were just Elim churches using the team for an evangelistic event. At other times, several churches got together for a major outreach event in a city. In each town, we would help to deliver 10,000 leaflets around the houses advertising the crusade and explaining that Jesus heals today by giving examples from stories we'd seen. We would spend a couple of weeks working with the church, putting in place prayer strategies, training people on how to deal with those who responded to the gospel appeal and how to pray for those who came forward for healing during the meetings. Then we would be part of the crusades' teams, helping wherever we could. Sometimes we were in the worship team, or in the ministry team, praying for people at the end of the meeting. Often, we would stay behind after the tents had gone back to Birkenhead and help the church to follow up all the contacts they had made during the week.

Booklets were produced using the *Journey into Life* tract (by Norman Warren) and Mark's Gospel. They were printed with the EET's logos and given out to anybody who made the decision to follow Jesus or showed an interest in becoming a Christian. Over the years we had thousands of these printed and distributed. We took the names and addresses of those people who responded and then, after the crusades, contacted them to encourage them to join a church or home group so they would grow in their faith.

We were involved in crusades in both small towns and large cities across the country. It was exciting to see multiple people coming to faith at these events. We knew that the months we spent preparing the high-quality publicity and literature had drawn many people in. It was not unusual to see the 300-seater marquee full by the last night of the crusade. The large marquee, that could accommodate up to 1200 people a night, was used for major city crusades. Again, it would regularly be full. It was so exciting to see people coming to faith, and not just one at a time, but twenty or thirty each night. People brought their friends and relatives, who people had been waiting years for a response, to hear the good news that Jesus can change lives. It may seem old-fashioned to see people coming forward for prayer, to see people be healed, and to see people celebrate the fact that Jesus transforms lives and heals today. To be involved in it was one of the greatest joys we could ever have experienced.

Over the years, we have seen God do some amazing things in people's lives. Let me explore a few stories out of the hundreds we have seen.

The biggest miracles are when someone comes to faith and recognises they are a sinner in need of a Saviour. They acknowledge that they have no answer in themselves and then turn to God for him to forgive them and restore their relationship with him. The Bible calls this being born again. That's a great way to think about it. Becoming a Christian isn't about going to church, it's about a new start. It's about turning away from our sin and towards him — we call this repentance. It's about a whole life change. Our past mistakes and attitudes all washed away; a new beginning, a fresh start, with God in his rightful place at the centre of our lives.

One night, the meeting was already underway. I saw two middle-aged men helping an elderly lady in a wheelchair through the rather awkward door to the venue. They began to gently move some of the chairs so she could sit on the back row in her wheelchair. It didn't just carry her but an oxygen cylinder. Plastic tubing snaked from it and went around her back and across her face. It was a sad sight, but she had come to the right place. We were on the Isle of Man. We had taken over the Floral Hall on the seafront at Douglas for one of our Gospel, Miracle and Healing Crusades that were happening for the whole week.

Leaflets had gone out across the whole island. All the churches came together, which was quite an unusual thing, but they all wanted to be involved in putting on this special event. This was our first evening and I was sitting at the back managing the sound system, trying to get the balance for the worship team. They were playing at the front, and it was my job to make it sound something nice and exciting, and then Paul got up to speak. He gave a very simple message explaining the need for people to come to faith in Jesus. He started to call people forwards, saying he was there to pray and to see people healed, restored and set free.

The lady in the wheelchair was one of the first to respond. She was pushed by her two sons to the front of the hall. I went and joined them as she explained to Paul that she was in the process of arranging a last meal for her family; she wanted to have them all together to say goodbye. She'd been told that the emphysema she had was fatal and there was no hope of recovery. She knew she only had a matter of weeks left and so was determined to make the best of it with her loved ones. We prayed for her. We saw no difference in her body and she left with her sons steering her down the aisle and out into the darkness of the night.

The following evening, she was back again. This time, only one of her sons was with her and she did look a little bit better. Sometimes, there are miraculous, instantaneous healings. At other times, it's just a gentle increase in health. Guess what? She was there every night throughout the week and every night we saw an improvement. She was still a ninety-year-old lady, but by the end of the week she was walking unaccompanied with no wheelchair, no oxygen, and she was able to sit in an ordinary chair with no assistance. The family knew it was a miracle. They went ahead with that special meal later that week, not to say a final farewell but to celebrate that they had their mum and grandmother back for a few more weeks, maybe even years. God is in the business of restoring relationships and our health.

One of our first experiences with the Healing Crusades was during a trip to Gambia with Paul, after only a few weeks of working with him. Getting off the plane was like walking into an oven. Ann has never been good with excessive heat and was already struggling when we arrived at our hotel, so I paid the additional premium for a room with air-conditioning.

The Gambia is an incredibly poor country with most of the population living on the breadline. The hotel, although one of the best in the country, was a budget hotel by our standards but it was on the beach. Our room quite quickly became the base for our operations. We were there with a small team, including another married couple; she was a GP and her husband was a consultant on the British Medical Council.

The team was asked by a group of local churches to do a crusade from a school building. The school was almost derelict, built with rough homemade bricks and no glass in the windows. One of the churches had a worship team, but they didn't have many instruments and their keyboard had several broken keys. And yet, night after night, the hall was full to overflowing. People were arriving hours early just to secure a place. I have never seen so many people wanting to encounter God, and the lines for prayer at the end of each meeting snaked around the hall and into the night.

Each of the team prayed alongside a local minister and every few minutes, David, the consultant doctor, would shout, 'Another one,' as another person was healed. Interestingly, many of those needing prayer from David and the local pastor were deaf. David didn't have any medical skills in that area but was blown away that God chose to work through him to restore their hearing.

Every night, as we arrived at the venue, there was a group of young people outside – begging. One young girl was in her late teens and was selling candles. She was disabled and wheelchair bound. We persuaded her to come into the meeting but, because of the crowds, the two doctors met her in an adjacent room. After examining her, they explained that she had malformed legs with no structure or strength. Every night, they prayed, and every day, they saw an improvement.

Her legs were gaining strength and muscle density. By the end of the week, she was able to stand.

The local pastors acted as our guides and chauffeurs. They were so poor that on payday, they could put a few gallons of petrol in their cars to drive and visit people. When they ran out of fuel, they would leave the car at the side of the road till the next pay packet. We were able to pay for all their fuel, which kept them on the road so they could visit their congregations.

On the Sunday, we were sent to different churches to preach. Ann and I went to a church with a congregation of a hundred or so. They sat in the open air, with a flimsy wooden frame supporting a tired tarpaulin to shield us from the sun. At the end of the meeting, after we had prayed with almost all the people there, they insisted on giving us a love gift to honour us. These poor folk had given out of their poverty to bless us. When we got back to the hotel and opened the envelope, there was enough to buy a glass of coke at the hotel prices. We wept as we realised what it had cost them. They wanted to honour God for all that he had been doing among them and they were so grateful.

It was a week that we will never forget. Hundreds came to faith, many were healed, and we worked with local churches and encouraged them. By doing that, we were so encouraged ourselves. When we came back to England, we continued to help them practically by collecting and sending over musical instruments to replace their broken ones.

Working for God is so exciting. Prayer really does work.

He limped into the meeting hardly able to walk. A big, strapping young man had been reduced to barely being able to walk. We were in Barking in London with our 300-seater tent. It was made with a striking blue and white canvas and so wasn't unlike a circus tent. With powder blue stacking chairs, a raised stage, a decent sound system, lighting and a generator, we transported it to various towns and cities on a 7.5 tonne lorry. In Barking, the local council had put stringent health and safety requirements on the Crusade, but we complied with every one of them; cabling was buried into the ground, and chairs firmly tied together.

Chris, as I will call him, was due to be a local steward to help people in and out of the meeting. Unfortunately, a nasty fall at work had injured his back and he was now seeking prayer. The next night, we could hardly believe our eyes. As we arrived early to set up, Chris was outside playing football with the local kids and encouraging them to come to the meeting. He was miraculously and totally healed. What a testimony he has. Chris later went on to join the ministry and is a church leader today.

Barking was an amazing crusade. One of the other incredible healings was a little girl, no more than two or three years old, who was severely disabled. For the first few nights, her dad sceptically brought her to the front of the healing line, but nothing changed. Pastor Paul would gently take her in his arms and pray for her. Ann was often standing with the family and watched as this little girl would turn her head from side to side, unable to focus on anything. The meetings were late for her so by the Friday night, she stayed at home but her dad came back. At the end of the meeting, he came forward as proxy for his daughter and we prayed with him. The time was approximately 9:20.

When he arrived home, he found his wife bubbling over with joy. Their little girl had been lying on her mat near the fire, listless, as usual. Suddenly, she sat up, reached out her arms and said 'Mama' for the first time. It was at 9:20. When they brought her to the meeting the following night, there was so much rejoicing. It had been such a memorable crusade.

That was Saturday, the last evening of the crusade, and we were staying on for the Sunday morning church service. We had been hoping that the family would come along to the service. Mum and the children did attend sporadically but always without Dad. We were rather saddened as the service started and they were not in the congregation. Half an hour later, the doors burst open and the entire family entered with the little girl walking in between her parents, holding each of their hands. Apparently, they had arrived at their usual bus stop and she'd demanded, 'No! Walk!' What a miracle. We visited the church some years later and saw the 'miracle girl' as part of the church youth group.

Chapter Nineteen

Native American Surprise

The firelight gave a beautiful glow to the faces gathered around the flames. They called it a campfire, but to me, it looked more like a low bonfire. It was over three metres wide, but only less than a metre high, so all of us could see across it. We were seated on a variety of things: camping chairs, wooden stools, rugs, blankets and cushions. We were there for the long haul.

They started building the fire at 5 o'clock, beginning by placing a circle of good-sized stones around the spot where the fire would be. Evenings, even in summer, could be quite chilly in north-west America.

As each camp finished eating, they brought out their chairs to form this large group of people sitting across from Ann and me. They didn't just bring seats. As I looked around, I saw all sorts of musical instruments: guitars, flutes, whistles, pipes, violins, accordions and, of course, lots of Native American drums. We had been surprised to see the variety of drums, from the small handheld Bodhran-type to the larger ones that sat between the player's legs and were hit with a drumstick. Not to mention the huge free-standing Pow-Wow drums that sometimes boomed out across the campsite.

This was the last night of an amazing week. We were in Oregon because our daughter, Rachel, was due to marry her American fiancé in a couple of weeks. Her future in-laws were part of an 1860s reenactment society who got together a few times a year. They lived together as folk had done in the nineteenth century – fur-trappers, settlers, traders, and Native Americans. Ann and I were invited to join them. Brought up on Cowboy and Indian films and loving everything to do with the American West, we jumped at the idea. And boy, did they make us feel welcome.

Our friends owned a tipi which they used on the Rendezvous, but we borrowed one from a Native American friend of theirs. There were bright blue and purple triangles that covered the bottom of the white canvas, with yellow stars above next to a huge yellow sun. The skull of a buffalo was depicted very realistically in grey, red and white on a turquoise square of cloth. This design was dotted across the whole canvas so it was very eye-catching. It looked dramatic; the mountains, stars, sun rays and buffalo skulls glowed brightly as they were caught by the sunset. It was amazing sleeping in the tipi, lying cosily warm at night, and being able to see the stars through the opening between the smoke flaps.

On the Rendezvous, we needed to look authentic. Rachel had secretly sent our measurements and had clothes made for us. Ann had a dark blue and green checked dress. It was a thick material and had long sleeves; it needed to be warm because even in the height of summer, the evenings became very cold. There were some blankets and ponchos to wear around the campfire too, but July could also have soaring temperatures during the day. So, Ann's second dress was pink and black striped cotton with white lace around the neck and short sleeves. Everything was a perfect fit.

Ann was very pleased with her gifts and I began to wonder about my own. They turned out to be two handmade shirts. The first was dark blue with tiny white spots all over it, and the other was dark red and covered in pale green leaves. They both had huge full sleeves caught into broad cuffs and had open necks with long, leather laces at the front. They also gave us moccasins; Ann's were what we might have been expecting, like suede slippers except with beadwork sewn on top, in turquoise, black and white. Mine, however, were quite different. The foot part was nearly the same but with no decoration and attached to them was more of the beautiful, soft tan leather to transform them into boots. Worn over trousers, with long, leather laces criss-crossing around my legs, they made a snug, comfortable fit. I didn't feel like I was wearing shoes at all.

When we got to the Rendezvous, there were already several smaller tents set up. Some were tipis, but others were square, white tents that looked like houses. They looked like little white houses, with four straight walls, a ridged roof and even a chimney at the back. There was a good mixture of people enthusiastically anticipating the week's activities; there were stall holders, families, some Christians, and others who were not yet believers.

That was the beginning of a memorable week; we even learnt to shoot black powder guns. They took us to a local range where we learnt how to load and fire the muzzle-loading rifles, replicas of those used in the nineteenth century. There was a tomahawk competition where we threw axes at a wooden target. We cooked over the open fire between the two tipis with cooking irons suspended over the flames. There, we prepared everything from burgers to 'biscuits in gravy' – a typical American breakfast of scones with a flavoursome sausage-based sauce. Then, finally, on

Independence Day, we participated in an incredible parade through the town led by mounted police. We joined the procession in our new period clothing, and several of us carried a black powder gun, which we fired skyward. Having loaded them with small pieces of silver foil as we fired them, they cascaded down all around us. The parade finished with an evening's firework display.

Our last night became a celebration and everyone gathered around the huge campfire. It was the way they traditionally ended their Rendezvous, singing songs accompanied by instruments. It gave it all a great sense of camaraderie. The songs were a mixture of folk, ballads and ones of faith. Some songs we knew, some were solos or instrumentals, but others were so well known that everyone joined in. What a beautiful, memorable evening.

As the sun was setting, there was a lull in the singing and another visitor arrived. Imagine a traditional Native American chief, about age fifty, well-built, carrying a headdress of eagle feathers and a commanding presence. Well, this visitor was exactly like that. He took his place in an open area of grass beside the fire. The drums were beating, low and slow, before building to a great crescendo. Slowly, he started to dance to the beat of the drums. As the tempo increased, he leapt and spun, wielding his staff high in the air with leather tassels flying until he dropped to his knees and held his arms high in his final gesture. Everyone applauded.

We were told he was a chief of the Black Foot tribe, who would occasionally join their Rendezvous. As he approached us, the chief removed his headdress. He also took off his large necklace, which had long leather tassels and was made from beads, some black or brass, but most were carved from bones. There were five strands of bone beads that formed the choker around the neck, and others snaked down towards a medallion hanging in the necklace's middle.

He walked straight over to Ann and said, 'God told me that I must give this to you. I was wounded for the love of my country.'

He pointed to what I thought was the decorative medallion, but it was the Purple Heart, the American military medal given to soldiers for outstanding service for their country after being killed or wounded in battle. He said God told him how Ann had been wounded because of her love of her husband; he said God wanted her to know that he saw her heartache and was walking with her through all the difficult times.

No one knew our history and as Ann began to gently explain, a sense of awe fell over the crowd. The Bible says God sees every tear that falls. In fact, Psalm 56:8 gives us a beautiful picture of him collecting our tears in his bottle. There is also a wonderful poem called 'Footprints' where the author walks across a beach and sees two sets of footprints. One set belongs to her and the other belongs to Jesus. She notices that during life's hardest moments, there's only one set of footprints. She asks Jesus why he has left her, but he responds that he never did – those were the times when he carried her.

We had to travel thousands of miles for someone to give this message to Ann. What an encouragement. She often tells this story when she preaches, especially in evangelistic settings, drawing three key thoughts together: the chief was wounded for the love of his country, Ann was wounded for the love of her husband, and someone was wounded because of his love for all people. It's our choice to respond to that love. What an amazing God we serve.

The mounted breastplate holds pride of place in our home to this day.

Chapter Twenty

The Goodness of God

It's never fun to be in hospital, especially when it's for your own child. We were worried. Scared. And away from home. The waiting room was crowded, noisy and unfamiliar.

We were downtown in one of the poorest districts in the centre of Nashville, Tennessee. Our daughter Rachel had moved to America at just nineteen-years-old to marry her American fiancé. Since their wedding, Justin was establishing himself as a drummer and record producer in Nashville, but his work was intermittent. As a result, Rachel was working fulltime as a nanny to support them.

By this time, after five incredible years with the EET, we felt the call of God to train at Bible college and were now pastoring in Essex. Ann had just finished a small Alpha course with ladies from a toddler group when Rachel rang. She was asking for prayer as the mother she worked for was pregnant again and wanted Rachel to prepare the nursery for the new baby. Justin and Rachel had now been married for several years, and though she was desperate for a baby, they were childless. She knew that having to prepare for another baby's arrival was going to be emotionally difficult. It just so happened that the topic on the Alpha course that day was whether God heals today. After talking about several miracles we'd seen while working with the EET, we finished the meeting with prayer and Ann felt to ask these girls, who weren't yet believers, to pray for Rachel. It was extremely moving as a small group of mums prayed for our daughter to have a baby of her own.

The following week, we were able to share how Rachel not only found the job easy to manage but she had enjoyed getting their things from the loft for the newly decorated nursery. Ann explained that sometimes God answers prayer in a different way to what we expect. The course finished and we went on holiday to Turkey, not knowing what would happen while we were there.

For several years, Ann and I enjoyed scuba diving. We spent the small inheritance from my parents on our own equipment and loved diving around the coast of Cornwall as well as seeing some amazing wrecks in the Red Sea. This was the first time we were diving in Turkey. We arrived at our hotel in a spectacular location, right on the coast, in the little town of Kes. It was a small, five-storey, ancient stone building. We ate breakfast in the open air from tables overlooking the bay, and the hotel had exclusive access to the sea via steep steps to decking that reached across the water. There was an old metal ladder down into the beautiful, deep water of the cove, where squid sheltered in the shade beneath the wooden planks. In the evening, the decking turned into the dining terrace, and we would eat the most delicious steaks as the sun set over the silhouette of the island of Rhodes a few miles away.

Scuba diving isn't a light activity when it comes to equipment. There are tanks, weight belts, wetsuits, BCDs (buoyancy control devices – inflatable vests used to control a diver's buoyancy underwater), regulators, masks and snorkels, boots and fins, dive watches, special torches and knives. It all made for a heavy load, and that was before our holiday luggage. As I mentioned, this was an old, stone hotel and we were assigned a room on the top floor. The owner apologised that due to the nature of the building, there was only a lift as far as the second floor, with a steep set of stairs then going up to our room. We looked at our baggage and dive gear, took a deep breath, and began the climb.

It's not safe to dive alone, but always with a 'buddy', just in case of any difficulty. This was our first time in Turkey, so we needed the services of a local guide, as even with a diving buddy everyone had to be accompanied so that no artefacts could be stolen by divers. Fortunately, the local guide had an office in the hotel, on the ground floor, so each day, we could leave the tanks there to be filled. Unfortunately, we had to haul the other gear up those stairs; we were feeling fit by the end of the holiday.

The divemaster guided us out on some wonderful daytime dives. We saw sunken villages, lots of sea creatures and even on one memorable occasion, the remains of a shipwreck from around 2000 years ago. As we were swimming along that day, she pointed to one amphora pot, then a few yards ahead, a couple more. Next, came five or six, mostly broken, but some with their typical rounded bases and beautiful handles intact. Amphorae are the large, clay jars that ancient people would use to transport foodstuffs from grain to wine and olives. The guide also showed us a round stone, about half a metre across with a hole carved into it – all that was left of the sea anchors. Finally, we came to the evidence of the shipwreck itself. Most of the wood and tackle was lost in the mists of time, but there, on the seabed, was a boat-shaped grouping of broken amphorae surrounding round stones and the ballast that kept the boat upright.

It was a sobering sight to see the remains of a ship lost at sea. It reminded us of the shipwreck that the Apostle Paul endured. The Bible tells us they began to throw the cargo overboard to lighten the boat before they then threw away the anchors as the storm grew worse. They hoped to ride it out, but as the waves grew larger and the winds blew harder, they even contemplated throwing the prisoners overboard too. However, Paul reassured them that God had told him they would all be safe, not a single person lost, and the Roman officer believed him. This proved to be the case; their ship was lost on the beach at Malta, but all the crew, the soldiers and the prisoners were unharmed. This exciting story is in Acts 27:11-44.

The daytime dives were amazing, but the ones we enjoyed the most were at night. We would meet the divemaster on the steps leading down to the harbour, where she explained how the dive would proceed. We would begin by swimming down the slipway along the harbour wall, slowly and carefully, with our eyes wide open. There were so many sea creatures who were nocturnal, sleeping through the day and coming out to feed in the darkness. We had our torches with us, and we would follow the guide, pausing to gaze in wonder as she identified anemone waving their tentacles, lionfish shimmering in the torchlight, squid quivering their arms, and to our joy, a small octopus hiding in the rocks. We wouldn't have noticed the octopus without her pointing it out as it was so well camouflaged. We enjoyed that night so much that we happily booked more nighttime dives with her.

One day, while we were diving, we heard an incredible noise, like one of those rattles people use to cheer for their team at a football match. Usually, diving is a quiet sport so we both looked up, wondering if there was a large boat passing overhead. To our amazement, the whole surface of the water was twinkling, shimmering as the raindrops of a torrential storm hammered down a few metres above us. The divemaster said we should stay underwater until the rain died down.

That night, we were in our bedroom on the top floor, looking out over the sea. The view was breathtaking, especially as the sky was lit with the most dramatic, dry lightning storm; sheets of brilliant blue-white streaked across the sky, while great tongues of forked shafts speared down and lit up the bay. We must have watched for about twenty minutes and then, the phone rang. It was Rachel. She told us she was expecting a baby. Our tears of joy matched the rain of the sky. We sent many prayers of thanksgiving up to our awesome creator and were so happy for them that we ended up dancing around the room to the rolls of thunder above us. It had been a truly incredible holiday.

On our return home, we forwarded $800 for Justin and Rachel to provide anti-natal care and then booked a flight to America. It just so happened that when we had only been there a few days, Rachel woke one morning with the news every pregnant girl dreads. She was bleeding. We rushed her straight to the hospital that was part of her anti-natal package.

So here we were, sitting, and waiting. Every few minutes, the alarm bells would ring, and another gunshot victim would be wheeled in. After what seemed like ages, Rachel was eventually called through, where she was seen by a doctor and sent home to be put on bed rest. The whole incident helped us all to make a decision – this was not the place we wanted the baby to be born. When her time came, Rachel would return to England and the baby would be born in an English hospital, and that is exactly what happened.

A few weeks before her due date, Rachel came and joined us in Essex. A week or so later, her best friend from Yorkshire, who just so happened to be a nurse, came to stay. We left the girls in the manse and drove to our little caravan, just fifteen miles away. At 3 a.m. the following morning, the phone rang, and Rachel was in labour and on the way to the hospital. Sophia was born three weeks early and had to spend the first few days of her life in an incubator. Once again, we were so glad Rachel had opted to have the baby here; she was only a few weeks old when they returned to America.

As parents, we always want the very best for our children. So we were devastated that when Sophia was just a few months old, Justin and Rachel could no longer afford the mortgage repayments on their house. Due to a downturn in the economy and a hike in interest rates, they were reduced to 'sofa surfing'. This meant they shared a house with a number of other couples and Sophia was sleeping in a built-in wardrobe in their small bedroom.

It is amazing to see God in the details. Ann and I decided that we would remortgage our house, taking out a loan which almost doubled our repayments, and use that money to buy a house in America. We were able to buy a small, detached bungalow on the outskirts of Nashville. It just so happened that on the day we transferred the money, the international interest rates mysteriously changed. A pound was worth more than $2, which was unheard of, and it only remained at that rate for a short time. This meant the money going into the escrow account was considerably more than we expected. We were able to use the extra money to renovate part of the house, replacing the roof and the bathroom.

A few years later, Rachel, Justin and Sophia relocated to England. It just so happened that when we came to sell the house and transfer the money back to the UK, the interest rates went the other way, and the dollars transferred into our UK account were again more than anticipated. God is so good.

By 2006, our son Phil was married with a couple of girls and a baby on the way. He had a poorly paid job as a taxi driver, and they were living in rented property in Liverpool. They were sharing the house with his mother-in-law and one of their sisters-in-law to keep expenses down and pay off debt. He was working as a volunteer youth worker in their local church.

One day, his wife had taken their two little toddlers to the stay-and-play group. It just so happened that on that morning, some television directors were visiting. They said they were making a 'fly on the wall' documentary and wondered if anyone would be willing to engage with them. The documentary followed a man from a rural community who had just moved to Liverpool, and they wanted to see how he coped living only on benefits in a big city. They had rented a flat for him and were going to follow him as he interacted with the community. Now at the play group, they were asking if anyone would be interested in being part of the programme.

Most of the mums didn't want to be involved, but Phil's wife did. A week later, the directors arrived, complete with camera crew and sound technicians, and this scruffy looking guy in an anorak and beanie. At the end of the session, Phil's mother-in-law invited the guy to church to meet others in the community and then to come back for Sunday lunch at their house with the whole family. Phil is a great cook, and Sunday lunch was one of his specialities.

Of course, this meant that the whole camera crew had to come too. They had lunch and then Phil sat chatting with the guy, recounting how difficult life was with not much money coming in, and him having to work long hours to make ends meet. The guy could see that Phil's extended family were living with him, and asked why they weren't on the housing ladder, as in the end, renting was throwing good money away. Phil explained that they had never been able to save up for a deposit, so there was little they could do about it. The guy said that he lived in a little village near Bishop Auckland, looking after sheep. He commiserated with them about the difficulty of life without a lot of money and thanked them for their generosity in providing him with a great meal and a chance to make new friends.

They didn't hear anything more from the team, until a couple of weeks later. Phil answered the door to find the 'shepherd' on his doorstep, with the camera crew again. This time, he was not in scruffy clothes, but an Armani suit. He smiled and said that he had a confession to make: in fact he was not penniless, but was a multimillionaire. He asked if he could come in. He explained that they were filming for a new series called *The Secret Millionaire.* He had deliberately come to the poorer part of the city to see if there was anyone that he could help. He had been touched by their story, but also by the care they had shown to a seemingly penniless stranger. He handed Phil a cheque for £10,000 to go towards a deposit for their first house and agreed to pay all the legal costs of the purchase.

This was a lifechanging moment for Phil as a few months later, he was able to move into his own home. The episode is still available on *YouTube* – Series One Episode Two of *The Secret Millionaire.*

Chapter Twenty-One

Making a Difference

'It's all your fault.'

I was at a funeral and these words were my welcome by a young man who I couldn't even place.

'I hope you realise it's all your fault that I am in ministry,' he added, laughing, 'I am an Anglican minister now.'

As the conversation flowed, I began to recognise him as one of the young people we encouraged years before. This was the second time in a few months that someone from our past had spoken to me out of the blue. The first was another young man we had mentored when our children were young. He contacted us through Facebook, inviting us to preach at his church. At that time, we had lost touch with him and didn't even realise he was in ministry. What a joy it was to catch up and witness God's hand of blessing on his life.

One of the greatest things about being a pastor is getting involved in people's lives. A pastor walks through heartaches with them and scales mountains of success by their side. He or she supports them, teaches them, encourages them, and sees them grow into what God has planned for them. After twenty-two years in the police, followed by five years with the Elim Evangelistic Team, we had felt God's calling to train for the ministry at Bible college, which led to another career, as we pastored in Essex for seventeen years.

I have previously mentioned that we have always encouraged those we trained to flourish in their own giftings. During my time in the police, we held holiday Bible clubs and as the youngsters grew older, we enabled them to move up to become assistant team leaders. We taught and developed them into a drama team to be proud of. Firstly, we used the drama team for the holiday Bible clubs, much to the joy of the younger children. Then we gave them the opportunity to perform in our schools' team events and later, to join our team who ran the after-school kids' club. Then, we took the drama team, with others, on a mission trip to Wales where our friend, an Anglican vicar, wanted to launch children's work in his church. Finally, we took the team with us as we ran a Scripture Union (SU) beach mission at Polzeath. In fact, one of our young people continued with SU every year for more than two decades after we had moved on. This proved to be excellent training for him before attending Bible college himself, and then becoming a paid youth leader.

During the time we were leading a church, we ran schools of evangelism and raised up a group of young leaders, whom we called our Young Lions. We trained up musicians, worship leaders, choirs and school teams and, in doing so, we have always tried to train leaders who could make these jobs their own.

As we write this, we have just returned from Elim's conference in Harrogate where all Elim ministers gather each year. It was great to catch up with John and Rene Young, who took over the leading of Leigh Elim Church when we retired. It is with their permission that we tell this story.

John was our elder at church, and he and Rene had owned a craft shop for several years in a local garden centre in Essex. They then had the opportunity to move into the town centre to expand their business. Perhaps they imagined that this move would be permanent, but God had other plans for their future, and who could have thought that they would be where they are today?

One Sunday, Rene came to church saddened because she had lost one of the diamonds out of her engagement ring. Despite thoroughly searching their home and the shop, they couldn't find it. It was hardly surprising as it was not the size of the Cullinan Diamond, but it was a tiny and well-loved little stone that captured the light beautifully in its various facets. After a few months, John bought her another diamond to replace it.

During the economic downturn, it became necessary to close the shop permanently. On their final day, Ann and I drove there to pray with them during this sad time, but also to encourage them that God hadn't finished with them. When one door closes, he opens another. We bought a few items from the closing down sale to encourage them, and then the four of us went into the upstairs office, now almost completely bare, to pray; it was quite an emotional time – the end of an era.

With an aching heart and a sense of sadness for our friends, we went down into the shop as they began dismantling the display stands and clearing out all the remaining stock – the papers and paints and glitter, so many little shiny beads and other bits and pieces that could be glued onto cards.

It just so happened that a bright shaft of sunlight seemed to catch something in the recesses of a dark area that had not seen the light of day for many months. Gingerly, I reached my finger into the darkness, only to draw it out immediately with a sharp intake of breath as pain caused me to pull my hand away. I bent down to get a better look, just as John lifted the cash register to load it into the van. What was it that was so small, yet glinted and seemed to hold the light? What was it that was so tiny, yet so sharp that it stabbed my finger?

I was stunned and couldn't believe what I was seeing. I said to Rene, 'Is this anything?'

'No,' she gasped loudly in amazement with tears welling up in her eyes. It was the missing diamond. What a miracle! I believe it was God's way of saying to them, 'You may think it's over, but I haven't forgotten you. I haven't finished with you yet.'

Since the engagement ring already had a replacement diamond, this precious stone, a wonderful reminder of God's goodness and his love, has been mounted into a beautiful silver pendant.

John's prophetic gifting developed in church and Rene's worship leading went to another level as she taught, trained and released others into worship ministry. John's job in management at a local supermarket and Rene's job as a care worker saw them go through Covid-19 as key workers. What better preparation for them to fulfil God's new plans? When Ann and I retired, we knew that God had placed them there 'for such a time as this' (Esther 4:14). They thought they were leading the church 'until a new pastor was appointed.' However, we were not in the least surprised when a couple of years later, the leaders of Elim asked John to become the pastor of Leigh Elim Church. This church is continuing to thrive under their oversight, all while they fulfil several other roles in the local area. That's what we call making a difference.

Chapter Twenty-Two

Final Twist?

A few years later, I was told I was dying. We were advised to prepare for an 'end of life' scenario.

We had been on holiday to Israel and seen some amazing sites, but I had started to feel slightly unwell. A few weeks later, after returning home, we went to our annual conference in Harrogate before staying on for an extra week's holiday. Despite being in a fabulous hotel, I just didn't feel right; I felt nauseous all the time. So, when we got home, I saw the doctor who sent me off for a blood test.

The next morning at 9 a.m., my doctor rang and told me to come straight down to the surgery. The blood test showed something abnormal, so he sent me to the kidney unit at the local hospital for another blood test. By 11.30 a.m. that same morning Ann and I were sitting in the consultant's room and were told that I had kidney failure and there was nothing they could do for me. I was admitted to the kidney ward to wait for the 'end'. To say I was shocked was an understatement.

OK, I hadn't felt well, but it wasn't anything dramatic, and suddenly, I was told my kidneys had failed. Imagine the effect this had on us, the family and our church. Phil and his wife rushed down from the Midlands to be with us; he immediately offered one of his kidneys, if that would help, and spent time praying for me. Rachel came to see me after getting special dispensation from the staff to bring her six-week-old twins with her.

It just so happened that the doctors had caught it in time and discovered that another less fatal issue was the reason my kidneys were failing. A few months later, by a small operation under local anaesthetic, they were able to put it right. Despite all the trauma we went through, can I see God's hand in this? I sure can. I see his hand in the fact that the problem was found in time, I see his hand in the knowledge and experience that the medical staff used to solve my problem, but I especially see his hand in the minutes and hours after the operation. I was taken to the recovery ward where the nurse in charge wasn't happy with my recovery. Instead of releasing me to another ward, she kept me in the recovery ward right through the night. This is not normal practice.

At 2 a.m., I was the only patient with three members of staff sitting next to me. The conversation moved to what I did for a living and then, why? For the next couple of hours, I shared some of my stories with the staff explaining how and why I was a Christian. One of the nurses, who was pregnant, explained that although she didn't go to church herself, she wanted her unborn child to go. I was able to encourage all of them to explore Jesus for themselves. If that was why I was ill, then I count it all joy, as it says in James' letter – 'Consider it pure joy, my brothers and sisters, whenever you face trials of many kinds' (James 1:2).

It's wonderful to share how amazing our God is, whether by writing these stories today, or through sharing them as God gives us opportunities in our everyday lives. I want to give him all the glory for taking an ordinary guy whose life was going nowhere particularly special to fulfilling his plans and purposes in that guy's everyday spaces. He is truly amazing.

Chapter Twenty-Three

Finding God in the Everyday

When we first started writing this book, Ann read a passage in her daily devotions. It talked about being reminded of all the times she had spent in the presence of God; the moments when his Word had directed her life and filled it with victory. It confirmed to us that we had landed on the theme for this book. About all those moments when 'it just so happened' – those life experiences which we'd later look back on and see God in the everyday. We wanted to share these moments, not just to entertain, but to help others see that God is at work in their lives too. Even in the small everyday situations. If we can see that he is there in those tiny details, then we can begin to trust him again, even with uncertain futures before us.

Sometimes, while we wait for big miracles or the fulfilment of great dreams and prophetic promises, we forget to see or even look for God in the seemingly insignificant parts of life. It's only when we look back that we see how it all fits together, like a jigsaw being completed with the hand of God putting down the pieces. The Bible frequently uses phrases like 'it just so happened', 'he arrived at a certain place' or 'it came to pass.' It could seem like things were happening by chance, but God was in every single event.

It's not the destination, but the journey that's important. That's where the lessons are. When we stop and analyse the journey, we see the obstacles we've overcome, and the faith and trust that have been strengthened along the way. The destination may have changed – from vice cop to vicar – but we have learnt and grown in ways we never could have imagined.

We should all think through our lives and remember some of those 'it just so happened' moments. There may be stories we want to share with friends and family to demonstrate the hand of God behind those decisions, circumstances and events.

We have mentioned numerous times how easy it is to take these things for granted. It is our prayer that many would be able to see God's hand in their lives and they would turn to him in praise and thanksgiving for the things that *just so happened*.

Acknowledgements

Wow, what an incredible journey we have been on as we've written this book. We want to thank every one of you who has listened to Derrick's stories, whether that's as part of a talk at church, over a meal with friends or simply sitting around chatting about life. All your comments and encouragements over the years set this project in motion, so thank you.

We would like to thank Malcolm Down Publishing for their help in turning this from Ann writing about Derrick's reminiscences into a story worth sharing.

We would like to express our deepest appreciation and thanks to Lydia Jenkins, our editor, for all her hard work and encouragement throughout this process.

It was a real surprise to see Esther Kotecha's work on the eye-catching cover; black for the police, white for ministry, but the appearance of a rip across the middle speaks to us of the heartbreak that went into Derrick's transition from Vice Cop to Vicar.

Above all, we want to thank our God who is, without doubt, with us in the everyday.